JRP|EDITIONS & LES PRESSES DU RÉEL

Alice Rawsthorn
Design as an Attitude

Table of Contents

PROLOGUE
Design as an Attitude

The Ocean Cleanup aims to tackle one of the world's biggest pollution problems by clearing plastic trash from the oceans.
Computer rendering of the system in action during trials in the North Sea, Europe.

Designing is not a profession but
an attitude.
—*László Moholy-Nagy*[1]

The new year did not start well.
Having spent six years wrestling
with financial crises and political
conflicts while struggling to establish a new design school in Chicago,
László Moholy-Nagy found himself at loggerheads with the board
again at the beginning of 1945: this
time over the dearth of students.
He also faced the challenge of finding new premises when the lease
on the school's building expired
that spring. The first school that
Moholy-Nagy opened in Chicago
had closed after little more than
a year, and the second was now
threatened by the same fate.
Eventually, he won over the board
and the school survived, but the
battle to save it took a brutal toll
on Moholy-Nagy himself.

He had hoped that 1945, when he
turned 50, would be the year when

he could devote more time to writing the book on visual theory he had begun two years before. But the school's problems proved so pernicious that Moholy-Nagy's days were filled with teaching and administration and his evenings were swamped by the commercial design projects with which he supported his family financially, leaving him with a few snatched hours at weekends to work on the book. To make matters worse, Moholy-Nagy fell seriously ill during the autumn of 1945, and was diagnosed with leukemia. Even after being admitted to hospital, he urged his wife Sibyl to bring portfolios of photographs, drawings, and notes on her visits so that he could work on layouts between blood transfusions, injections, and X-rays.[2]

Moholy-Nagy was discharged just before Christmas, and resumed his duties at the school the following month. He seized every free moment during the spring and summer to finish the book, but his condition deteriorated, and he died on November 24, 1946.[3] His book, *Vision in Motion*, was published the following year. No one reading it then, or now, would be likely to guess what a dreadful ordeal its author had experienced while writing it. As a manifesto of Moholy-Nagy's vision of design, art, technology, creative education, and their roles in society, it distills the ideas and observations of a remarkably gifted and dynamic individual, who had experienced the birth of constructivism in his native Hungary after World War I, the heyday of the Bauhaus in 1920s Germany, and the emergence of modernism during the 1930s, first in Britain and then in the United States. Even though Moholy-Nagy was gravely ill while writing *Vision in Motion*, the book resounds with his energy and optimism, especially with regard to his belief in design's power to build a better world.

This eclectic and empowering vision of design, and the passionate conviction that society could benefit from adopting a more open-minded and progressive approach to it is summed up in Chapter Two of *Vision in Motion* with the words: "Designing is not a profession but an attitude." I have always loved that phrase, quaint though the reference to "designing" sounds today. "The idea of design and the profession of the designer has to be transformed from the notion of a specialist function into a generally valid attitude of resourcefulness and inventiveness which allows projects to be seen not in isolation but in relationship with the need of the individual and the community," Moholy-Nagy wrote. "Ultimately all problems of design merge into one great problem: 'design for life.' In a healthy society, this design for life will encourage every profession and vocation to play its part since the degree of relatedness to all their work gives to any civilization its quality."[4]

Liberating design from the constraints of the professional role it had occupied since the Industrial Revolution by redefining it as an improvisational medium rooted in instinct, ingenuity, and resourcefulness, and open to everyone, was typical of Moholy-Nagy. Intrepid, generous, subversive, and irrepressibly curious, he is one of my favorite characters in design history. Who could resist the émigré artist and intellectual, who wore a factory worker's boiler suit to signify his zest for technology while teaching at the Bauhaus, where he allowed women to study whatever they wished, including subjects previously reserved for men? And who would not admire Moholy-Nagy's courage after his arrival in the United States? His new daily uniform was a business suit, yet he remained as radical as ever in his politics, notably by welcoming African-Americans to his Chicago design school in an era when the city's education system was largely segregated. Wherever he was, and regardless of his personal circumstances, Moholy-Nagy sustained his enthusiasm for experimentation: from pioneering the then-new media of film and photography, to investigating their impact on visual culture and every other aspect of daily life.

Moholy-Nagy's concept of design as an attitude was rooted in his youthful commitment to the constructivist movement, which he encountered as a young artist in Budapest immediately after Word War I. Design played a pivotal role in the work of the original constructivists, the group of avant-garde Russian artists, writers, and intellectuals, who met to exchange ideas and plan social change in the final years of the war, and included Aleksandr Rodchenko, his wife Varvara Stepanova, and their friends, Aleksei Gan, El Lissitzky, and Lyubov Popova. Their belief that artists, designers, and scientists should work in collaboration with industry to build a better, fairer society, by creating "new things for the new life" as Popova put it, was shared by the constructivist sympathizers who Moholy-Nagy encountered while living in Vienna and Berlin during the early 1920s.

This was the vision of design that Moholy-Nagy introduced to the Bauhaus after his arrival in March 1923. Over the next five years, he emerged as the school's most influential teacher, and was instrumental in positioning it as a progressive and inclusive institution, steeped in experimentation. After leaving the Bauhaus in 1928, Moholy-Nagy imbued all of his new ventures, including the Chicago schools, with the same spirit, which he articulated brilliantly in the concept of attitudinal design described in *Vision in Motion*.

This book is entitled *Design as an Attitude* partly in tribute to Moholy-Nagy, but also because those words sum up much of the work it describes. *Design as an Attitude* is based on the *By Design* columns I wrote from 2014 to 2017 for the art magazine *frieze* as a survey of what I consider to be the most important issues in contemporary design. My objective is to portray what, I believe, is an exhilarating, though intensely challenging period for design, when the discipline itself and its impact on our lives are changing dramatically.

As design has adopted so many different meanings at different times and in different contexts, and been prone to muddles and clichés, it seems sensible to begin by defining what I believe it is. In all of its manifold guises, design has always had one elemental role as an agent of change that interprets shifts of any type—social, political, economic, scientific, technological, cultural, ecological, or whatever—to ensure that they will affect us positively, rather than negatively. *Design as an Attitude* explores how designers, professional and otherwise, are fulfilling this role at an extraordinarily turbulent, often perilous time when we face changes of unprecedented speed and scale on many fronts.

Among these are global challenges like the environmental emergency and refugee crisis; the rise of poverty, prejudice, intolerance, and extremism; the recognition that many of

the systems and institutions, which organized our lives in
the last century, are no longer effective; and the torrent of
ever more complex and powerful technologies that promise
to transform society, though not always for the better.
Design as an Attitude describes how designers are responding
by planning and executing projects to tackle climate change;
to reinvent dysfunctional areas of health care and social
services; to provide emergency support for the victims of
man-made and natural disasters; to help asylum seekers to
settle into new communities; and to champion social justice.
It charts the evolution of design's relationship to other
disciplines, such as art and craft, and its role in the resurgence of interest in making, whether by hand, mechanically,
or digitally. The book also maps the recent shifts in design
culture as it becomes more diverse and inclusive, not only
in terms of gender, geography and ethnicity, but by embracing people from very different fields, who did not train to
be designers, yet are eager to engage with design.

Technological change is a recurrent theme. As well as
assessing the successes and failures of design's record in
developing applications for once bafflingly futuristic, now
ubiquitous technologies such as smartphones, social media,
blockchains, and biometric identification software, *Design
as an Attitude* anticipates the impact of artificial intelligence,
quantum computing, driverless cars, digital fabrication,
and the other advances that we know will affect us in the near
future. How are such innovations changing what we need
and want from design? And how will they affect our expecta-
tions of the level of choice and control we wish to exercise
in different aspects of our lives, and our ability to express
our increasingly fluid, nuanced, and idiosyncratic personal
identities?

Not all of the projects described in the book have been
executed by the type of attitudinal designers described by
Moholy-Nagy, but many of them were. In defining design
as "an attitude," Moholy-Nagy recognized its potential to
become a more powerful force in society by acting as an
efficient and ingenious agent of change, free from commercial constraints. There have always been designers who
have done this: Rodchenko, Stepanova, El Lissitzky, Popova,

and Gan were among them, as was Moholy-Nagy himself. So was the maverick US designer, engineer, architect, and activist R. Buckminster Fuller, who inveighed against the environmental damage caused by industrialization as early as the 1920s, and devoted his working life to assuaging it. Fuller also flung himself into designing practical solutions to the housing shortage during and after World War II by developing prefabricated structures to be built swiftly and safely. During the 1960s and 1970s he mounted a campaign to mobilize a global movement of "comprehensive design- ers" who, he hoped, would forsake commercialism to devote their skills to forging a better future, and sounded remark- ably like Moholy-Nagy's attitudinalists.

Design has also been deployed as an eloquent form of politi- cal protest. Young French artists and designers occupied the École des Beaux-Arts in Paris during the May 1968 student revolt to establish the Atelier Populaire, where they produced hundreds of posters as what they called "weapons in the service of the struggle." A different cause benefited from the resourcefulness of the anonymous members of Gran Fury, a collective that designed banners, billboards, T-shirts, and stickers to raise awareness of AIDS worldwide, and to challenge misconceptions about it during the late 1980s and early 1990s. Typical of Gran Fury's work was a series of posters bearing the apt and memorable slogan: "Kissing Doesn't Kill: Greed and Indifference Do."

Inspiring though such projects are, attitudinal design remained on the margins of the design community through- out the 20th century. Yet the last decade has seen a radical transformation of design into the fluid, open-ended medium described in *Vision in Motion*.

The chief catalyst—apart from the determination and vigor of the individuals concerned—is the plethora of digital tools that have transformed the practice and possibilities of design. Most of these technologies are fairly basic and inexpensive, but, if imaginatively applied, can be remarkably useful in helping designers to operate independently. The availability of crowdfunding platforms, for example, makes it possible for them to raise capital. (The possibility

of securing grants from the growing number of charitable
foundations that support social and humanitarian design
projects, including Acumen, the Bill and Melinda Gates
Foundation, and The Kendeda Fund, helps too.) Designers
are also able to manage huge quantities of complex data
on affordable computers, and to use social media to raise
awareness of their work in order to flush out collaborators,
suppliers, and fabricators, and to clinch funding or generate
media coverage. Individually, each of these changes would
have had a positive impact on design culture, but collectively they have proved metamorphic. Today's attitudinal
designers also benefit from the growing recognition that
established methodologies are no longer fit for purpose in
acutely important fields, including social services, health
care, economic development, and disaster relief, making the
specialists in those sectors increasingly amenable to trying
new approaches.

Not that every designer will turn attitudinal; nor should they.
Many of them will continue to study and practice specialist
disciplines—such as automotive, fashion, graphic, interior,
product, software, or user experience design—in the conventional way, and to work in commercial environments.
The lucky ones will find this work enjoyable, challenging,
productive, and worthwhile. Some of them will contribute
to the commercial design programs that are driving social
and environmental progress, such as the development
of more efficient systems of generating clean, renewable
energy.[5] Yet more and more designers will seize the oppor-
tunity to pursue their political, cultural, and ecological
concerns by operating independently. They will also seek
to define their own idiosyncratic ways of working, often in
collaboration with other specialists, such as artists, programmers, economists, politicians, anthropologists, social
scientists, psychologists, or statisticians. Conversely, those
communities will be readier to engage with design, just as
Moholy-Nagy envisaged.

The next chapter will describe what attitudinal design means
in practice, but here are two examples. The first is one of
the boldest, and most mediatized projects so far: the Ocean
Cleanup, a Dutch non-profit which is dedicated to addressing

one of the world's biggest pollution problems by clearing
the mass of plastic trash that is poisoning the oceans. It was
founded in 2013 by a 19-year-old design engineering student
Boyan Slat, after he discovered more plastic bags in the water
than fish on a diving holiday in Greece. The Ocean Cleanup
began by raising $2.2 million from crowdfunding to devise
a giant floating structure with which Slat hoped to collect,
contain, and clear plastic trash from the huge garbage patches
that have congregated in the Pacific. His plans have been
criticized by scientists and environmentalists alike, yet he
succeeded in securing more than $30 million to complete
the prototyping and initial testing of the system, and to start
advanced trials in the Pacific Ocean in 2018.

Equally ambitious, though less conspicuous, is Sehat Kahani,
a project that has already had a significant impact on the
quality of health care for Pakistani women thanks to the
instinctive design flair of two doctors, Sara Khurram and
Iffat Zafar. Pakistan suffers from a severe shortage of women
doctors, even though three out of four of the country's
medical graduates are female. Many of them marry shortly
after graduation, and come under intense social and family
pressure to stop working, as Khurram did when she was
forced to leave her job after becoming pregnant. As a result,
there is a grave scarcity of female doctors to care for
Pakistani women, many of whom do not wish to be treated
by men. Working with the Pakistani social entrepreneur
Asher Hasan, Khurram and Zafar developed a network of
teleclinics to enable female doctors to practice from their
homes by examining women patients on live video links.
The doctors liaise with the female nurses and community
health workers in the clinics, who arrange the patients'
treatment. The concept, originally named DoctHERS, was
tested in the Sultanabad area of Karachi in 2014, before
expanding into other urban areas and rural regions, where
medical resources are even scarcer. Khurram, Zafar, and
their colleagues encountered many problems—ranging from
inadequate electricity supplies in rural clinics, to convincing
skeptical, technophobic patients that the doctor speaking
to them on the screen was qualified to treat them—but they
managed to find solutions. They now plan to expand Sehat
Kahani's network throughout the country.

A teleconsultation between a doctor and patient at Sehat Kahani's E-Hub, Model Colony, Karachi, Pakistan. Sehat Kahani is establishing a telemedical network throughout Pakistan to enable women and girls to be diagnosed online by female doctors.

Design has not traditionally been seen as an obvious solution to health care shortages or plastic pollution. Nor were independent designers expected to raise as much start-up capital as $30 million to mount epic ecological ventures on the scale of the Ocean Cleanup, or doctors, like Khurram and Zafar, to recognize that design could prove useful to their work. Even now, more people are likely to perceive design as a styling device, or as a reason why so much plastic trash is poisoning the oceans, rather than as a means of clearing it away. If Moholy-Nagy's vision of "design for life" is to be realized, those stereotypes must be squashed. The only way to do this is for design, attitudinal and otherwise, to prove its worth in other spheres. Why else would politicians, bureaucrats, and NGOs consider it to be capable of helping the victims of war crimes to secure justice, or to develop more efficient global systems of managing digital waste? And why would doctors continue to experiment with it? Design will only be empowered to play a more prominent and potent role in our lives if it demonstrates that it deserves to do so, by being deployed wisely and sensitively with the "generally valid attitude of resourcefulness and inventiveness" described in *Vision in Motion*.[6]

[1] László Moholy-Nagy, *Vision in Motion*, Paul Theobald & Co., Chicago, Illinois 1947, p. 42.

[2] Sibyl Moholy-Nagy, *Moholy-Nagy: Experiment in Totality*, Harper & Brothers, New York 1950, p. 213–223.

[3] Ibid., p. 247.

[4] László Moholy-Nagy, *Vision in Motion*,. p. 42.

[5] In his talk "The Case for Optimism on Climate Change" at TED 2016 in Vancouver, Al Gore identified one of the principal causes for optimism being the unexpectedly high increase in production of clean, renewable energy, and its declining cost. Gore explained that over 20 times more wind power was being generated at the time of his speech than had been forecast when he delivered his lecture "An Inconvenient Truth" in 2006. He also explained that nearly 70 times more solar power was being generated, thereby enabling us to consume less fossil fuel. Al Gore, "The Case for Optimism on Climate Change," TED Talk, https://www.ted.com/talks/al_gore_the_case_for_optimism_on_climate_change.

[6] László Moholy-Nagy, *Vision in Motion*, p. 42.

CHAPTER I
What Is Attitudinal Design?

Arthur Zang has designed the Cardiopad, a mobile heart monitor, which promises to improve the quality of health care in rural Cameroon and other countries.

Too often, the role of the designer
is to clothe a set of messages they've
had no participation in. Here is a
book. You didn't write it. You don't
change it except insofar as you
present the information somebody
else has generated. You're not really
collaborating, either, because the
stuff is here, an accomplished fact.
I decided I had to wash that out
of my head.
—*Muriel Cooper*[1]

If any designer can be said to per-
sonify design as an attitude, it is
Willem Sandberg. As director of the
Stedelijk Museum in Amsterdam
from 1945 to 1962, Sandberg not only
established it as one of the most
dynamic cultural institutions of the
postwar era by championing new
movements in art, and introducing
design and photography to the
collection, he also discharged an
unofficial, unpaid role as its graphic
designer. Working late into the
night and scribbling under the table
at board meetings, he designed

hundreds of exhibition catalogues and posters, as well as all of the Stedelijk's stationery and tickets. Sandberg prided himself on the economy of his graphics. Many of the posters were purely typographic, made from the small selection of typefaces available at Amsterdam's municipal printworks, never in more than three colors, one of which was always red. Yet his compositions were so deft, with adroit contrasts of colors and typefaces, that his designs were elegant, engaging, and wholly appropriate to the theme of every exhibition.

Had his reputation rested solely on his graphics for the Stedelijk, Sandberg would be celebrated as a talented, modernist designer, but he achieved much more than that by deploying design to very different ends. As the son of a wealthy Dutch family, Sandberg, who was born in 1897, led a charmed youth among the European intelligentsia. After studying art in Amsterdam for a year, he spent time with avant-garde groups in Austria, France, and Germany, and worked in a Swiss printshop, where he became fascinated by typography. Returning to Amsterdam in 1928, he opened a graphic design studio and started working for the Stedelijk. Sandberg's advice on the content of the exhibitions proved so incisive that the museum hired him as a curator in 1937. The following year, he organized the *Abstract Art* exhibition, one of the first surveys of the subject by a major international museum. But his life changed radically during World War II, after Germany invaded the Netherlands in 1940, and he joined the Dutch Resistance, where he found new applications for his design skills.

During the early years of the German occupation, Sandberg used his graphic dexterity and knowledge of typography to forge identity papers for hundreds of Jews, political dissidents, and others threatened by persecution. The fake documents were printed on Sundays at a print works owned by one of his closest friends and Resistance colleagues, Frans Duwaer. Sandberg's forgeries were so convincing that most of the people he helped successfully evaded arrest. (He later described this as "the greatest praise I ever had for typographical work.") Yet there was one foolproof way for the Gestapo to verify whether identity papers were bogus— by checking them against the official documents stored in the Amsterdam Public Records Office. Desperate to prevent this from happening, Sandberg and four friends hatched a plan in 1943 to set the Public Records Office on fire and destroy its contents. They were betrayed to the Gestapo, and went into hiding.

One by one, most of Sandberg's coconspirators were captured and executed. He survived by living quietly in the southern and eastern Netherlands, under the alias of Henri Willem van den Bosch. Barely subsisting at a time of severe food shortages, Sandberg lived in terror of capture, haunted by the knowledge that many of his friends were already dead, his wife was in prison, and their son in a concentration camp. Having drawn on his design prowess to save so many lives in his work for the Resistance, he turned to it to help him to withstand the lonely, precarious existence of a fugitive. From December 1943 until April 1945, Sandberg began the process of designing and prototyping a series of 19 pamphlets that he called *Experimenta Typographica*.

Each pamphlet was roughly 15 by 20 centimeters in size, and consisted of up to 60 pages of drawings, collages, typographic exercises, and texts written by Sandberg or one of his favorite writers, including the novelist Stendhal and the political philosopher Pierre-Joseph Proudhon. Sandberg made several copies of each one from whatever materials he could find: mostly scraps of paper and cardboard picked up off the street, wallpaper swatches, or pages torn from magazines. Every edition was devoted to a theme that intrigued him and had influenced his work before the war, such as architecture, death, education, love, and typography. Producing the first issues of *Experimenta Typographica* was fraught with danger. Frans Duwaer agreed to print them, but was arrested and killed by the Gestapo. The pamphlets were eventually printed by a printshop known as the Vijpondpers, or "five pound press" in a reference to the Nazi ban on publications that required more than five pounds of paper.[2] By immersing himself in a prolonged design process steeped in the ideas and values he had treasured before the war, the *Experimenta Typographica* project gave Sandberg the courage to cope with living in dread of losing his own life and those of the people he cherished.

When the war ended, he returned to Amsterdam, where he was reunited with his wife and son, and appointed director of the Stedelijk. Sandberg's subsequent design work for the museum benefited from the precision and technical ingenuity of his forgeries for the Resistance, and the joyful frugality of *Experimenta Typographica*. By deploying design not only as a cultural tool, but as a defense against human rights abuses and a deeply personal medium of self-expression, he served as an exemplar of László Moholy-Nagy's vision of attitudinal design.

Yet design had been practiced in that way for centuries, long before a word was coined to describe it, or Moholy-Nagy sought to redefine it. Whenever human beings have adapted to changes in their lives—whether by fabricating new objects or structures, or developing ways of moderating their own behavior or other people's—they have engaged with design, but have done so intuitively, often unconsciously. Prehistoric men and women acted as designers by sharpening sticks and stones to make them more useful as farming tools, or by molding clay into vessels to be eaten or drunk from. So did the Ancient Egyptians when they embarked on epic endeavors, like the construction of colossal pyramids as part of elaborate death rituals, or on intimate projects, such as the design and fabrication of a meticulously crafted wooden and leather artificial toe. Discovered in 1997 by the archaeologists who were excavating a burial chamber near Luxor, the ancient prosthetic is believed to have been custom-made for a wealthy woman over three thousand years ago.[3]

Many subsequent design feats have been equally instinctive. The white flag was officially acknowledged as a symbol of surrender by the Hague Conventions of 1899 and 1907, but had been used for that purpose as early as the Eastern Han Dynasty in the first century AD. The raised fist has been recognized as a sign of strength and unity in the face of adversity for over four thousand years since being identified as an emblem of Ishtar, the Mesopotamian goddess of love, sex, and war. The same symbol has been adopted by a succession of political activists, from campaigners for workers' rights in the early 1900s, to the members of the

Black Power and women's movements of the 1960s and
1970s, and, more recently, Black Lives Matter.

Improvisational design coups have also fuelled economic
success. Take the city of Venice, whose inhabitants have
fought to defy the laws of physics and nature: first by building a city on the tiny mud islands of the Laguna Venezia in
the fifth century; and then by defending it against the threat
of erosion, humidity, pollution, and flooding. To do so,
they designed innovative methods of construction and repair,
starting with the tree trunks they shipped to Venice from
Slovenia and drove deep into the mud to hoist the city above
the water. By the late 1600s, Venice had become the richest
and most sophisticated city in Europe, with an empire
stretching nearly as far west as Milan, and across the sea
to Cyprus, thanks in no small part to the design prowess of
the Arsenale shipyard. Hailed as the most efficient manufacturing complex of the age, the Arsenale occupied over
a hundred acres of land, roughly an eighth of the city. It
owed its success to the efficiency with which several genera-
tions of Venetian naval engineers had speeded up production without compromising the quality of the finished ships.
Specific areas of the site were designated to specialize in
making cabins, rigging, and other parts of the vessels; and
the design of each component was standardized in the
interests of speed and precision. Partially-built ships floated
from area to area along the canals that coursed through
the Arsenale. By the early 16th century, this system was so
robust that the Arsenale could accommodate as many as
a hundred ships at once, and was capable of building a basic
vessel in a few hours and kitting it out with state-of-the-
art weapons by the end of the day, providing a formidable
fleet to defend and enlarge the Venetian empire.

Nor did design lose its prehistoric "necessity is the mother
of invention" role as a useful tool for resourceful people
in challenging circumstances. When the 19th-century health
care reformer Florence Nightingale volunteered to work
in the British Army's military clinics in Turkey during the
Crimean War, she was horrified to discover that more patients
were dying from infections contracted in the filthy wards
than from battle wounds. Nightingale drew on the research

of a doctor and social reformer working in Manchester, John Roberton, who had designed model hospitals and convalescent homes with cleanliness and safety in mind. She adapted his design principles for military use, and lobbied the government for funding to implement them, becoming an early champion of information design by drawing cleverly illustrated pie charts to communicate her arguments clearly and convincingly. Back in Britain after the war, Nightingale deployed a similar design strategy in a new campaign to construct larger, more hygienic, and better-equipped civilian hospitals.

By then, the design process had been applied, knowingly and systematically for over a century to manufacture huge quantities of goods of consistent quality. The practice of design had also been formalized and professionalized with the introduction of training programs, specialist schools, clearly defined categories, and methodologies. Despite the efforts of Moholy-Nagy, Buckminster Fuller, l'Atelier Populaire, Gran Fury, Sandberg, and fellow attitudinalists, design has continued to be seen predominantly in this industrial guise as a profession. Thanks to their new digital tools, today's designers have been liberated and empowered to work autonomously in the attitudinal spirit advocated by Moholy-Nagy. What are they doing with their newfound freedom?

In *Vision in Motion*, Moholy-Nagy identified the defining qualities of attitudinal design. One was to interpret design as an "attitude of resourcefulness and inventiveness," rather than as a formal process. Another was the conviction that design should be applied to major issues of the time: to the daunting social, political, environmental, and economic challenges that *The Economist* calls the "Big Problems." Moholy-Nagy also believed that attitudinal designers should be bold enough to identify the causes they wished to embrace, while being sufficiently open-minded to draw on the expertise of people in other fields, and to empower them to immerse themselves in design.

Boyan Slat, Sara Khurram, and Iffat Zafar fit the bill perfectly, as do a host of other attitudinal designers who are wrestling with equally urgent challenges. Take Brave New Alps, a design group founded in the Italian Tyrol in 2005 by Bianca Elzenbaumer and Fabio Franz. They have planned and executed social design projects that address the political and economic tensions of local communities throughout Italy, typically working with fellow designers and collaborators from other spheres. In 2016, they helped to open QuerciaLAB, a maker space in the Alpine town of Rovereto that provides training in carpentry and other skills, as well as tools, for local people and the asylum seekers who are trying to forge new lives in the region. Brave New Alps then joined forces with fellow activists to mount a crowdfunding campaign to finance Hospital(ity), a new venture intended to provide medical and legal support, as well as training resources for another vulnerable group of people, the migrant crop pickers living in what a local priest described as "inhuman and desperate conditions" in Rosarno, a town in southern Italy with a brutal recent history of racial conflict.

Another attitudinal project takes on extreme situations using very different methodologies. Forensic Architecture is a design research agency run by the Israeli architect Eyal Weizman at Goldsmiths, University of London, which seeks to secure justice for the victims of climate and war crimes, and other human rights abuses. Working with coders, lawyers, archaeologists, and scientists, the agency analyzes data from diverse sources, including cellphone records and architectural plans, to uncover the truth about such catastrophes as a devastating attack on a Syrian hospital, and why 63 migrants were left to die on a boat drifting in the central Mediterranean. Forensic Architecture also reconstructs such incidents by designing digital models and animations to be used as evidence in official investigations, policy reviews, and legal cases.[4]

Neither Forensic Architecture nor Brave New Alps could have executed such courageous, ambitious, and deeply personal design programs without the digital tools that have fueled the surge of activity in attitudinal design. The same applies to the new generation of designers now working in the African countries, where more people have access to cellular networks than to clean running water. Africa is

seldom mentioned in orthodox accounts of 20th-century
design history, yet the design cultures of Burkina Faso,
Ghana, Kenya, Mali, Nigeria, and other African nations are
now being transformed by technologies that are opening
them up to people who were hitherto excluded by a dearth
of training or investment, often both.

African designers are already at the forefront of developments in Internet of Things technologies in which information is exchanged between interconnected networks. Several
of them are designing medical products, which are intended
to improve the health care of people living in remote rural
areas, hundreds of miles from well-equipped hospitals with
specialist staff. The Cameroonian software designer Arthur
Zang has adapted a tablet computer to create a mobile heart
monitor, the Cardiopad, with which local nurses and para-
medics can check patients' hearts and send the data online
to a distant hospital for analysis. The diagnosis is sent
back with recommendations for treatment, thereby sparing
patients from arduous, expensive, potentially pointless
journeys. A group of doctors and designers in Kenya has
applied a similar principle in another portable digital device,
Peek Retina, which identifies eye problems. By making it
so much faster and easier for patients to be diagnosed and
treated, these products promise to help millions of people
not only in Cameroon and Kenya, but in other countries too.

Design's newfound accessibility is embracing people from
different disciplines, like the Kenyan doctors who helped
to develop Peek Retina and their Pakistani counterparts in
Sehat Kahani. Another convert is the British social scientist
Hilary Cottam, who has used design as a tool in her quest
to reinvent the welfare state for the 21st century. Traditionally, a designer's role in tackling societal problems like
unemployment, homelessness, and the difficulties of the
rapidly expanding elderly population was limited to producing websites or brochures explaining what social scientists,
politicians, and economists had decided to do, but Cottam
has embedded designers in the decision-making process.
She has assembled cross-disciplinary teams that are led by
designers and have applied the design process to analyze
complex social challenges, and to devise alternative

responses. One project replaced the relatively expensive and wasteful standardized packages of care that a local council in London was offering to elderly residents with a customized system, whereby the seniors living in each area of the borough contributed their knowledge and skills to help their peers, rather than passively receiving support from others. This design template has been replicated by similar programs throughout Britain, and Cottam's work has influenced other social design groups worldwide.

There are countless other applications for attitudinal design as subsequent chapters will relate: from the conceptual designers who treat the design process as a means of research and intellectual enquiry, like the Italian designers Studio Formafantasma's investigation into the global trade in digital and electronic waste, to ecological design adventurers. There are also traces of an attitudinal spirit among corporate design teams. The 1,000-plus designers employed worldwide by Nike have free rein to use an experimental space, the Blue Ribbon Studio, in the heart of its global headquarters in Beaverton, Oregon, where they find carpentry and metalwork tools, 3D printers, dyeing vats, stonewashing kit, *ikebana* classes, and several thousand books on art, architecture, and design. Fuseproject, IDEO, and other commercial design consultancies encourage their employees to experiment with *pro bono* projects to complement other assignments. Not that their motives—or Nike's—are entirely devoid of self-interest. Such experiments often flush out interesting and unexpected ideas for commercial projects, and not only encourage sought-after design graduates to join those firms, but may dissuade them from defecting to rival companies. Fuseproject has also applied attitudinal zest to the commercial side of design by forging what it calls design ventures with fledgling businesses by reducing its design fees in exchange for retaining an equity stake or royalties in the resulting products.

Inevitably, not all attitudinal design endeavors have been successful. Humanitarian design programs, like those of Brave New Alps and Forensic Architecture, can be as challenging and contentious as every other area of economic development. Sustainable design has proved equally stormy, as the Ocean Cleanup has discovered[5]; and even some of the most successful exercises in social design, including Cottam's experiments, have been imperiled by sudden political changes, such as government policy reforms or public funding cuts. Attitudinal design is a work in progress, and may well continue to be. Even so, the benefits of opening up design to new fields and different people with diverse skills are already apparent, as Willem Sandberg demonstrated so conclusively.

[1]   Janet Abrams, "Muriel Cooper," https://www.aiga.org/
        medalist-murielcooper.
[2]   Ank Leeuw Marcar (ed.), *Willem Sandberg – Portrait of an
        Artist*, Valiz, Amsterdam 2014.
[3]   Jason Daley, "This 3,000-Year-Old Wooden Toe Shows
        Early Artistry of Prosthetics," *Smithsonian.com*, June 21,
        2017, https://www.smithsonianmag.com/smart-news/
        study-reveals-secrets-ancient-cairo-toe-180963783.

[4]   Eyal Weizman, *Forensic Architecture: Violence at the Threshold of
        Detectability*, The MIT Press, Cambridge, Massachusetts
        2017.
[5]   Lindsey Kratochwill, "Too Good to Be True? The Ocean
        Cleanup Project Faces Feasibility Questions,"
        The Guardian, March 26, 2016.
        https://www.theguardian.com/environment/2016/mar/26/
        ocean-cleanup-project-environment-pollution-boyan-slat.

Detail of an office cubicle made from recycled digital and electronic waste by Studio Formafantasma as part of the 2017 Ore
Streams design research project into the global digital waste trade.
Commissioned by the National Gallery of Victoria, Melbourne, Australia, for the NVG Triennial, 2017.

CHAPTER 2
Spot the Difference:
Design and Art

In *The Pale Fox*, 2014, the French artist Camille Henrot explored the impact of digital information and imagery on how we see and interpret the world.

If people understand there's no
need to explain. If they don't,
there's no use explaining.
—*Jean Prouvé*

There are toxic words in every
field, and when it comes to design,
two of the most ominous are
"sculptural" and "artistic." Not that
there is necessarily anything wrong
with design projects exhibiting
either quality, but those that are
described as doing so seldom do.
Instead, they are very likely to be
any or all of the following: bland,
silly, blingy, pretentious, derivative,
ridiculous, or unjustifiably expensive. Check out the dodgier booths
at a "design-art" fair to see what
I mean.

If "sculptural" and "artistic" were
simply guilty of being inaccurate
and unwittingly pejorative, it would
be tempting to end the argument
by citing a favorite exchange in an
earlyish episode of *Game of Thrones*
in which the fabulously ghastly

Tywin Lannister parries his (just ghastly) grandson Joffrey
Baratheon's "I am the king, I will punish you," with a brusque
"Any man who must say, 'I am the king,' is no true king."
But, sadly, those adjectives are more damaging, because they
also foster the assumption that design is somehow elevated
by being likened to art. (It is true that applying the language
of art can help "design-art" dealers to convince impres-
sionable collectors to pay more money for their wares, but
that is another matter.) Design is not inferior to art, just
different. But how exactly do the disciplines differ at a time
when artists and art institutions are increasingly absorbed
by design, and when it is becoming ever more difficult to
distinguish the critiques of design culture made by designers,
from those of artists?

Historically, there was no perceived difference between
them. Both design and art were lumped together in what
the Ancient Greeks called *technê*, alongside craft, medicine,
and music. It was not until the Renaissance that a distinction emerged and artists were accorded higher social
and cultural status than designers and artisans. When
the first art school, the Accademia e Compagnia delle Arti
del Disegno, opened in Florence in 1563, art and design
were studied separately. Other schools followed suit, or
focused their teaching on art, and sometimes architecture,
while ignoring design.

The gulf between the disciplines widened during the industrial revolution when the practice of design was formalized as
a means of enabling manufacturers to produce huge quantities of more or less identical goods. In the early industrial
age, factories, like Josiah Wedgwood and Miles Mason's
potteries, were considered so thrilling that London intellectuals and socialites conducted manufacturing tours
of northern England and the Midlands.[1] Canny industrialists
made the most of their allure by persuading famous artists
to work for them, as Wedgwood did by commissioning
George Stubbs and John Flaxman to create ornamental
patterns for his pots. Tellingly, both artists are often
described as having "designed" for Wedgwood, when all
they really did was decorate his wares. The most important
design decisions, relating to the technical specifications

and choice of materials, glazes, and firing techniques, were made by Wedgwood himself and his modelers, mostly local boys from humble backgrounds, who had trained with him as teenage apprentices.[2]

By the early 1800s, the infatuation with industry was fading, and the demonology of "dark satanic mills" began. Manufacturing and everything associated with it was derided as filthy, noxious, shoddy, and destructive. The artists that once clamored to work for Wedgwood and his ilk were replaced by "designer-draftsmen," who were mostly poorly paid, powerless, and confined to copying historic symbols from books. The museums, which were founded to raise standards of design in manufacturing, including the Victoria & Albert Museum in London in 1852 and the Museum of Applied Arts in Vienna in 1864, tended to favor the decorative arts. The growing antipathy toward industry was crystallized by the increasingly popular arts and crafts movement, which championed a revival of rural craftsmanship. Even the efforts of as gifted an industrial designer as Christopher Dresser, who developed thoughtful and nuanced products by conducting exhaustive studies of different materials, production techniques, historic styles, and the strengths and weaknesses of the workshops that fabricated his designs, made little impact on the popular cliché of design as a supine tool of commerce.

The constructivists challenged that cliché during the 1910s by advocating a more enlightened understanding of design's potential to create a fairer, more productive society: first in Eastern Europe, then further afield as László Moholy-Nagy, El Lissitzky, and other members of the movement settled in other countries. By the 1930s, progressive art curators such as Alexander Dorner of the Landesmuseum in Hanover, were experimenting with design. The architect-turned-curator Philip Johnson did the same at The Museum of Modern Art in New York by displaying pistons, springs, ball bearings, propellers, and other examples of industrial beauty in the 1934 exhibition *Machine Art*. The critics savaged the show, but Johnson acquired a hundred of the exhibits as the beginning of what would become The Museum of Modern Art's celebrated design collection.

More modern art museums embraced design in the postwar
era including the forerunner of the Centre Pompidou in
Paris, and the Stedelijk Museum in Amsterdam during
Willem Sandberg's directorship. Like Johnson, the curators
of those institutions tended to focus on the visual dimension
of industrial design. Not that they were unjustified in doing
so, especially when the objects were as beguiling as the
beautifully resolved electronic products devised by Ettore
Sottsass for Olivetti and Dieter Rams for Braun in the late
1950s and 1960s, but other arguably more important elements
of their design, such as its cultural and environmental
impact and its relationship to technological change, were
often neglected.

Even the most radical attempts to interrogate design's
influence on contemporary culture focused on its role within
consumerism, like *This Is Tomorrow*, the multidisciplinary
exhibition organized by the Independent Group of artists,
architects, and designers, that opened at the Whitechapel
Gallery in London in 1956 with Robby the Robot from the
sci-fi movie *Forbidden Planet* in attendance. Richard Hamilton,
one of the artists in the show, conducted rigorous investigations into the design of cars and kitchen appliances, and
the construction of fashion imagery throughout his career.
He also made sculpture from mass market totems including
false teeth and electric toothbrushes, and filled paintings
with images of robots, toasters, comic books, corporate
logos, Hollywood stars, and other commercial iconography.
Serious and sophisticated though Hamilton's interest in
design was, it concentrated on its stylistic qualities and
populist affects.[3] So did the work of other artists with an
equally considered approach to design, including Ed Ruscha
in the United States and Isa Genzken in Germany. Ruscha
catalogued commercial graphics and vernacular buildings
in his paintings and photographs, while Genzken explored
the role of fashion, technology, and trash in consumer
culture. The same stereotypes were reinforced by much of
the late 20th-century critical discourse on design, such as
the essays of the British critic Reyner Banham,[4] and the
French philosophers Roland Barthes[5] and Jean Baudrillard.[6]

Collectively, these artists and writers sustained the popular misconception of design as a styling device, which was deployed to commercial ends, regardless of the environmental or ethical consequences, while emphasizing the compromised nature of the design process. Artists were widely perceived as being free to express themselves in work, which was often, though not always, of their own making; whereas designers were regarded as being impeded by countless obstacles from the demands of clients and fabricators, to the practical constraints of developing things that would be robust enough to withstand daily use.

Even the idea that design was only worthy of cultural consideration if it was deemed visually pleasing was demeaning. It linked design to the antiquated notion of art as striving for perfection at a time when progressive artists were intent on exploring the messier, darker, troubling aspects of life: something that seemed alien to a quest for mass-manufactured beauty. No wonder that when the Welsh cultural theorist Raymond Williams identified the words used most often to discuss British culture and society in his 1976 book *Keywords*, design was not among them, nor was it mentioned in the 1983 expanded edition.[7]

Design is no longer so easily ignored, principally because of the rise of attitudinal design and the accompanying changes in design practice that have enabled designers in every field to define their own objectives and to exercise greater control over their work. As we have seen, design has become more expressive and polemical, and readier to address complex social, political, and ecological challenges. Even its traditional applications, such as the interpretation of scientific and technological breakthroughs, have acquired a renewed urgency.

So compelling has design become that a growing number of art institutions have expanded their engagement with it: from the Kunsthalle Vienna, the Serpentine Galleries in London, the Van Abbemuseum in Eindhoven and the National Gallery of Victoria in Melbourne, to Artists Space, the New Museum and the Metropolitan Museum of Art in New York. Artists too are increasingly interested in

interrogating design and its impact on society. Ed Atkins,
Ian Cheng, Helen Marten, Yuri Pattison, Magali Reus, James
Richards, and Jordan Wolfson are among the artists who
have made their names internationally in recent years by
exploring the impact of digital technology on the ways we
relate to the world. The French artist Camille Henrot has
explored how our immersion in digital imagery and information is affecting our relationship to objects in installations
such as *The Pale Fox* at Chisenhale Gallery in London in 2014,
the self-explanatorily entitled *Office of Unreplied Emails* at
the 2016 Berlin Biennale for Contemporary Art, and *Days are
Dogs* at the Palais de Tokyo in Paris in 2017. The fetishistic
nonsense of over-programmed digital devices and their
superfluous functions has been satirized by the British artist
Mark Leckey in his ongoing project *GreenScreenRefrigerator*.
An important strand of the work of the German artist
Wolfgang Tillmans has been to analyze and document the
evolution of the objects, spaces, and structures we encoun-
ter daily in photographs of door keys, digital interfaces,
and car headlights.

Designers are pursuing similar objectives by using their
work as a research exercise to interrogate design's role as a
powerful, if sometimes problematic force in our lives. Would
you expect an artist or a designer to explore the impact
of colonialism and racism on craft tradition? The African-
American artist and activist Theaster Gates has done so in
studio pottery workshops and his investigations into the role
of ethnicity in the ceramics of Dave Drake and the ficti-
tious potter, Shoji Yamaguchi. So have the designers Simone
Farresin and Andrea Trimarchi of Studio Formafantasma
in 2009's *Moulding Tradition*, a ceramic project that explores
the legacy of the Muslim conquest of Sicily in the ninth
and tenth centuries in the context of the rise of racism in
contemporary Italy. Another common theme for artists and
designers is the mythology of mid-20th-century modernism,
notably the work of the Italian furniture designer Carlo
Mollino, which has been addressed by both the Iranian-born
artist Nairy Baghramian and the Italian designer-maker,
Martino Gamper.

Throughout his career, the German artist Wolfgang Tillmans has charted design's relationship to daily life in photographic works like *Headlight (f)*, 2012, that interrogate technocratic, mass-manufactured products.

How do the artists' responses differ from those of the designers? Not at all, at least not in terms of what really matters, because they are all fearless, perceptive, original, and provocative, yet there are also clear distinctions between them. One is that all of the design projects have a functional outcome: usable pots for Formafantasma; tables and chairs for Gamper in 2008's *Martino with Carlo Mollino*. Some of the ceramics made in Gates' workshops were usable too, but not all of his projects were intended to have practical functions, nor was Baghramian's 2011 project *Tea Room*, which was inspired by the surrealist installation *Tea No. 2* designed by Mollino in 1935. As artists, she and Gates were free to choose, unlike designers for whom functionality is compulsory. Not that their work necessarily needs to be functional in the practical sense, as *Moulding Tradition* and Gamper's study of Mollino's furniture happen to be, because the definition of function in design is becoming ever more fluid.

Another essential quality of a design project is that it must relate to design culture to some degree: whether through the application of the design process, or by making references in the finished work to design, whether they are historic or contemporary. Just as the experience of designing and making the pots in *Moulding Tradition* was integral to the evolution of Formafantasma's thinking, Gamper analyzed his subject by constructing new furniture from discarded components of Mollino's pieces. Only by doing so could he scrutinize the minutiae of their fabrication, whereas Baghramian studied Mollino's work by reinterpreting it in a different medium.

Even so, does it matter whether a work that explores a similar theme equally adroitly is described as art or design? Clearly it does to anyone with a strategic reason for choosing a particular discipline, like Theaster Gates, whose decision to identify himself as an artist enables him to sell work through commercial galleries in order to raise the necessary funds to finance his community housing program in Chicago. But there are also generic arguments in favor of sustaining the distinction.

One is that interrogating design's impact on society is a valuable exercise, as it would be for any ubiquitous force, which affects every area of our lives, especially one that is as prone to muddles, misconceptions, and clichés as design. Designers have a particular perspective to bring to that process, but so do artists, and both approaches are useful in their respective ways.

Moreover, if you believe that design is more than a styling tool, and has the potential to make a useful contribution to society by helping, say, to arrest the environmental or refugee crises, then it follows that we need the best possible designers. The more eclectic, dynamic, challenging, and attitudinal design practice appears to be, the likelier it will be to attract them, which is why it is not only wrong, but self-defeating to describe design in words that suggest it may be subservient to art.

[1]   Jenny Uglow, *The Lunar Men: The Friends who Made the Future 1730–1810*, Faber and Faber, London 2002, p. 49–52.

[2]   Alison Kelly (ed.), *The Story of Wedgwood* (1962), Faber & Faber, London 1975, p. 34.

[3]   Alice Rawsthorn, "Richard Hamilton and Design," in Mark Godfrey (ed.) *Richard Hamilton*, Tate Publishing, London 2014, p. 125–134.

[4]   Penny Sparke (ed.), *Reyner Banham, Design by Choice*, Academy Editions, London 1981.

[5]   Roland Barthes, *Mythologies* (1957) trans. Annette Lavers, Paladin, Frogmore, St. Albans 1973.

[6]   Jean Baudrillard, *The System of Objects* (1968), trans. James Benedict, Verso, London 2005.

[7]   Raymond Williams, *Keywords: A Vocabulary of Culture and Society* (1976), Fontana (Flamingo edition), London 1983.

CHAPTER 3
The Craft Revival

The resurgence of interest in craft and making has prompted the opening of maker spaces as places where designers, artists, makers, and enthusiasts can attend courses in design and making techniques, as well as use the tools, machinery, and other resources. Blackhorse Workshop in Walthamstow, northeast London, is one of the many maker spaces to have opened in recent years.

Diversity and inclusiveness are our only hope. It is not possible to plaster everything over with clean elegance. Dirty architecture, fuzzy theory, and dirty design must also be out there.

—*Sheila Levrant de Bretteville*[1]

They downed over a million soft drinks and scoffed nearly as many Bath buns, but most of the six million people who trooped into the Crystal Palace in London's Hyde Park to visit the Great Exhibition of the Works of Industry of all Nations in the summer of 1851 were drawn by prize exhibits like the world's biggest diamond, Gobelins tapestries, a demonstration of the cotton manufacturing process, and the first public toilets. The novelist Charlotte Brontë was so impressed that she described it as being "like a mighty Vanity Fair … very fine, gorgeous, animated, bewildering" in a letter to her father.[2]

One young Londoner took a frostier view. When the 17-year-old William Morris and his siblings were taken to the Great Exhibition as a treat by their mother, the rest of the family went in cheerfully, but he refused to join them. Convinced that he would loathe the Crystal Palace and its contents, the teenage medievalist and future champion of the arts and crafts movement, insisted on remaining outside where he sat sullenly on a chair, waiting until his family was ready to leave.[3]

Morris later discovered more eloquent ways of expressing his contempt for what he considered to be the soullessness and shoddiness of industrialization, notably in the rough-hewn "protest furniture" he designed in the mid-1850s in a medieval style for the rooms he shared with the artist Edward Burne-Jones. Yet his adolescent strop outside the Great Exhibition's orgy of consumerism summed up the relationship of design and craft for decades to come. Morris was not the only member of the craft community to consider design to be fatally compromised by its codependence on commerce and mechanization. Conversely, there was no shortage of designers who felt equally vociferously that their "raffia mafia" critics were twee and anachronistic.

Hostilities recently ceased, on one side at least, as designers have come to see craft in a different light: as more subtle, dynamic, and diverse than they previously thought it to be. Some designers have made strategic use of artisanal symbolism, as the Dutch product designer Hella Jongerius has done by giving mass-manufactured objects the appearance— or illusion—of the idiosyncrasies we have traditionally associated with handcraftsmanship. Others, like Jongerius' compatriot Christien Meindertsma, and the Italian duo Simone Farresin and Andrea Trimarchi of Studio Formafantasma, have explored the expressive qualities of the craft process, and its role in addressing social, political, and environmental issues. Does this growing interest represent a significant change in the design community's understanding of craft, and its cultural value? And is it accompanied by an equally radical shift within craft circles?

It is difficult to overstate how pernicious the battle between design and craft has been. Up until the industrial revolution

in the late 1700s, most objects were made by hand, often
by local blacksmiths or carpenters. Their skills were
widely admired, and in the early years of industrialization,
manufacturing was accorded similar respect. Celina Fox's
book *The Arts of Industry in the Age of Enlightenment* describes
how manufacturers vied for prizes for the most impres-
sive machinery at packed public exhibitions.[4] But by the
19th century, industry was blighted by its association with
labor exploitation, tackily made goods, urban squalor, and
the despoliation of the countryside. Morris, John Ruskin,
and fellow members of the Arts and Crafts movement fueled
these stereotypes in their writing and lectures, which
advocated a return to the supposedly gentler, purer values
of craftsmanship. Neither cliché was entirely accurate.
Some handcrafted wares were no less shoddy than the
tawdrier factory goods, while the finest industrial artifacts
matched the highest standards of craftsmanship.

Even so, the Arts and Crafts lobby was so persuasive that
its dogma survived into the early 20th century, proving
particularly virulent in Britain, Japan, Scandinavia, and the
United States. By then, constructivism was gathering force
in Eastern Europe, fired by its very different vision of design
and technology. Up until László Moholy-Nagy's arrival at
the Bauhaus in 1923, the school had adhered to a manifesto
that began: "Architects, sculptors, painters. We must all turn
to the crafts!" Moholy-Nagy soon converted his colleagues
to constructivism, and the Bauhaus' director Walter Gropius
coined a new slogan, "Art and Technology: A New Unity."
The Bauhaus' reinvention marked a turning point in the
cultural fortunes of craft and design, beginning a process
that shifted the balance of power firmly in the latter's favor.

By the mid-1950s, when Roland Barthes described "a super-
lative object" in an essay published in his book *Mythologies*,
he was referring, not to one of the painstakingly crafted
artifacts beloved of Morris and Ruskin, but to Citröen's
new DS 19 saloon.[5] A decade later, when Richard Hamilton
praised the objects that "have come to occupy a place in
my heart and consciousness that the Mont Saint-Victoire
did in Cézanne's" in an exhibition text, he was talking about
Braun's electronic products.[6]

Craft still had its champions, notably in Scandinavia and
Japan, where even modernist designers expressed their love
of the artisanal heritage and natural beauty of their countries
in the formal qualities of their work. The furniture designed
by the Finnish architects Alvar Aalto and Aino Maria
Marsio-Aalto in the 1930s has been manufactured from the
wood of birch trees growing in the same forest ever since.
Their fellow Finn, Tapio Wirkkala, developed spectacularly
beautiful glassware to be made at the Iittala glassworks
in Helsinki in shapes that evoked the swirling water of
Finland's fjords, and the icicles of its winters. The relationship between Japanese industrial design and craft was less
explicit, and was reflected in the shared values of simplicity,
efficiency, subtlety, and durability. Those are the qualities
that Sōetsu Yanagi, a young art historian, prized in the
examples of rural craftsmanship he discovered when traveling in the Japanese countryside during the mid-1920s.
Yanagi was so inspired that he founded the *mingei* movement
of like-minded artists, artisans, and intellectuals.[7] His
son, Sori, valued the same qualities, but applied them in
an industrial context in postwar Japan. As the designer
of hundreds of mass-manufactured products from vehicles
and cooking pots to soy sauce bottles, Sori Yanagi proved
that *mingei*'s values were robust enough to be interpreted
by different production technologies.

The politicians and designers responsible for the more
enlightened efforts to modernize national design cultures
took note. When the Cuban furniture designer Clara Porset
was invited to curate the exhibition *Art in Daily Life: Well-
Designed Objects Made in Mexico* at the Palacio de Bellas Artes
in Mexico City in 1952 as a manifesto for the future of
Mexican design, she combined factory wares with hand-
crafted objects found on rural research trips.[8] Porset was
convinced that the modernization of Mexican design should
be rooted in the country's rich artisanal heritage, which,
she believed, would not survive if it remained isolated from
modernity. The US industrial designers Charles and Ray
Eames came to a similar conclusion after being commissioned by the Indian government to conduct a national
design review in 1958. Their India Report concluded that
Indian industrial design should aspire to delivering the

same "tremendous service, dignity, and love" as the *lota*, a traditional water jug used daily in many Indian homes that the Eameses deemed to be "perhaps the greatest, the most beautiful" of all the objects "we have seen or admired during our visit to India."[9]

Yet Porset and the Eameses were in a minority, as design's cultural currency was rising, and craft's was falling. Craft also suffered from misogyny, having long been regarded as a female preserve. For decades, women had been encouraged to study so-called "feminine" subjects like ceramics and weaving, even at supposedly progressive art and design schools. During the Bauhaus' early years of craft evangelism, both Anni Albers and Gunta Stölzl were forced to abandon their original plans to join the glass making and architecture courses respectively, and to enroll in the weaving workshop, or "women's class." They are now regarded as two of the most influential textile designers of the 20th century, yet both felt impeded in different ways by being confined to a relatively obscure and financially precarious area of design. Like so many other things perceived as female, craft was marginalized.

Equally problematic was the dismissal of the craft traditions of developing countries, even those with proud artisanal histories, on the grounds that they might impede modernization. In India, despite the efforts of the Eameses and other craft enthusiasts, the critical reputations of designers and artists whose work was associated with artisanal symbolism or techniques—such as the potter Devi Prasad, and Mrinalini Mukherjee, who made sculpture from hemp and other textile materials—suffered from this misassumption.

No more. These days, designers drop craft references with alacrity, and design graduation shows are replete with investigations into artisanal history. The change began in the mid-1990s when Hella Jongerius, Jurgen Bey, and other young Dutch designers, who exhibited together as Droog Design, incorporated craft symbolism or techniques in their work. Typically, they did so to imbue mass-manufactured objects with the endearing or eccentric qualities of craftsmanship. Jongerius has programmed the production of factory-made ceramics to add the flaws we expect of handmade pots and to "sign" them with her fingerprint as master potters have done for centuries. She has achieved a similarly subversive effect in large-scale industrial design projects, including KLM's aircraft cabins, through the tactical use of embroidery, straggling threads, mismatched fabrics and other artisanal tropes.

Other designers have adopted a conceptual or anthropological approach to craft. Christien Meindertsma's projects have ranged from finding new uses for traditional artisanal materials like with The Flax Project, to celebrating one woman's achievement in knitting more than five hundred sweaters and identifying potentially valuable materials for recycling from the bottom ash salvaged from an incinerator. Studio Formafantasma has explored various episodes of Italian craft history including the use of lava from Mount Etna by Sicilian artisans to construct objects, and the ritual of bread making in rural communities. A popular strand of the annual Vienna Design Week is the Passionsweg program in which young designers develop new products in collaboration with venerable Viennese manufacturers, artisans, and workshops. The objective of pairing, say, the Swiss designer Adrien Rovero with the Posenanski Leather Manufacturer, or his Polish counterpart, Matylda Krzykowski, with the brush maker Norbert Meier and horn specialist Thomas Petz, is to introduce those designers to the creative possibilities of Viennese craftsmanship, while raising public awareness of the skills and ingenuity of the city's artisanal and industrial heritages. In Japan, even such technocratic designers as Naoto Fukasawa and Jasper Morrison have acknowledged the influence of *mingei* on their work. Fukasawa combines his industrial design practice with the directorship of Mingeikan, the Japan Folk Craft Museum, which was founded by Sōetsu Yanagi on the outskirts of Tokyo in 1936 to house his lovingly assembled collection of *mingei*.

Craft has enjoyed a similar renaissance among artists, many of whom now regularly engage with ceramics and other artisanal processes. Disappointing though it was in many respects, *Viva Arte Viva*, the main exhibition of the 2017 Venice Art Biennale curated by Christine Macel, was a resounding vindication of craft's growing importance within the visual arts. There has also been a critical reassessment of the work of artists whose association with craft was once considered pejorative, including Mukherjee's hemp sculptures and Sheila Hicks' textile installations, one of which was exhibited in *Viva Arte Viva*.

What happened? Why are once-dowdy words like "crafted," "artisanal," and "heritage" now ubiquitous in advertising campaigns? Why have YouTube film clips of potters working at their wheels become so popular? Why are new craft courses opening at art and design schools? Why do celebrity potters, like Grayson Perry and Edmund de Waal, command ever-higher prices for their work? And why did women all over the world choose to knit pink woolen hats with pointy feline ears to wear as symbols of political protest?

One explanation is that, after decades of admiring what once seemed like the heroic achievements of standardization and mass manufacturing, we now take their benefits for granted, and find it harder to ignore their shortcomings. We also know too much about the dark side of globalization to be unaware of its consequences. Just as factory wares summoned bleak visions of exploited child labor to William Morris in the late 1800s, it is difficult for us to look at, say, an Apple or Samsung smart phone without worrying whether it may have been made from conflict minerals by the poorly paid employees of an abusive subcontractor, or imagining it failing to biodegrade on a toxic landfill site. Tellingly, two of the most compelling public design projects of recent years— Norway's new banknotes, designed by Snøhetta and The Metric System, and the country's new passport, devised by Neue—depict the natural beauty of the Norwegian landscape, and traditional occupations, like farming and fishing, as well as the oil industry, which has been the primary source of the country's wealth since the 1980s. The delicate illustrations of Norway's forests and fjords on the pages of Neue's passport transform under ultraviolet light into a depiction of the Northern Lights shining in the night sky.

In an age when we devote so much of our time to devouring digital information and imagery on screens, perhaps it is inevitable that the spontaneity of craftsmanship should seem appealing. The same desire has fueled the popularity of concerts, festivals, debates, and other live events, as well as D.I.Y. activities such as gardening, knitting, and baking. The sociologist Richard Sennett redefined the intellectual framework of craftsmanship in his 2008 book *The Craftsman* by opening it up to include laboratory technicians and virtuoso musicians as well as weavers and glass blowers. Citing the medical research into the impact on the brain of the heightened sense of "active touch" developed by people who work with their hands to a high level of skill and dexterity, Sennett made an eloquent case for how pleasurable and empowering the physical experience of making things by hand can be.[10] Likewise, while many women's rights campaigners are happy to buy pink pussyhats to wear on marches, those that knit them for themselves, or for friends, say that the act of doing so deepens their commitment to the cause.

The artisanal revival also reflects the role of digital technology in reinventing the practice of design and craft. Traditionally, a key difference was that artisans were involved in making all or part of their work, whereas designers devised specifications and issued instructions as to how it should be made. The explosion of interest in all forms of making has eroded this distinction by encouraging more and more designers to adopt the roles traditionally fulfilled by craftspeople by fabricating all or part of their work themselves, and to focus on repairing existing objects and systems, as well as on developing new ones.

Critically, making is an integral part of one of the most dynamic areas of contemporary design, software programming. The process of typing instructions into a computer in the form of code combines design and making. It can also be argued that software designers conform to the arts and crafts movement's definition of craftspeople being dedicated individuals, who apply their skills by hand, albeit with a computer mouse and keyboard, rather than a carpenter's chisel or potter's wheel. If you accept this logic, it follows that software design embraces both craft and making, acting as a persuasive practical example of the possibilities of integrating all three activities, not only in that field, but in others too.

Another catalyst is the availability of increasingly sophisticated digital production technologies, such as 3D printing systems, which are so fast and precise that they have made it easier and less expensive for designers to make or customize all or part of new products, and also to repair old ones. The surge of interest in mending or fixing has been also stimulated by environmental concerns and the desire to prevent unnecessary consumption. A lively community of makers and fixers has emerged that embraces all forms of production, and prizes the output of skilled industrial fabricators as much as it does exquisite hand-sewn embroidery or impeccably constructed dry stone walls. Maker Spaces, Hacker Spaces, and Maker Libraries have sprung up to provide tools and training resources; as have Maker Assemblies and Maker Faires to enable the exchange of ideas and to exhibit makers' work. The Israeli-born designer and curator Daniel Charny has established Fixperts as a global network of designers, makers, and repairers, who experiment with new approaches; and the template of Make Works, a directory of factories, workshops, and any other Scottish makers that are interested in collaborating with designers run by the Glasgow-based design entrepreneur, Fi Scott, is being replicated in other regions.

Some of the new generation of African designers have integrated making and skill-sharing into their work from the outset. The schools, library, and other public buildings designed by Diébédo Francis Kéré in Gando, the village where he was born in central Burkina Faso, were constructed by a collective effort that required local people to learn new skills, including brickmaking. As well as hoping that their training will help some of those people to find sustainable employment, Kéré believes that by participating in the construction process, they will feel a closer attachment to the completed buildings. The Malian textile designer Boubacar Doumbia built his workshop Le Ndomo in Ségou, as a place where he could experiment with weaving and natural dyeing techniques, while training young people whose lack of education had made it hard to find employment.

Doumbia hopes that the trainees will also learn the life skills of discipline, diligence, and a sense of responsibility that should help them in whatever they eventually choose to do.

All of these changes have enlivened design practice, and have helped it to adapt to the challenges of postindustrial culture. Craft has benefited too, both from an injection of new thinking, and forays into dynamic new fields, such as software. Even so, it is debatable whether there has been the same degree of experimentation within established craft disciplines as there has been among the designers and artists who have ventured into their terrain; perhaps not yet.

There are encouraging precedents in the work of innovative practitioners like the British ceramicist Clare Twomey, whose research into artisanal history and the involvement of local communities in pottery embraces elements of art, design, anthropology, and craft. To mark the opening of the Centre of Ceramic Art in York in 2015, she produced *Manifest: 10,000 Hours*, a colossal installation of 10,000 ceramic bowls, one for each of the 10,000 hours traditionally deemed necessary to train a master craftsman. Each bowl was made by hand by one of hundreds of volunteers, mostly in York, giving each of them a stake in a work, which was to go on public display. Twomey embarked on another project to encourage the public to make pots in *Factory*, at Tate Modern in London in 2017. She began by opening an industrial pottery, where people clocked in, as they would in a traditional factory, and learnt how to work with clay. The future of craft may well be determined by its ability to embrace the elasticity of contemporary culture by making tactical incursions into other disciplines, as its old foe design has done so deftly.

[1] Ellen Lupton, "Reputations: Sheila Levrant de Bretteville," *Eye*, Autumn 1993.

[2] Charlotte Brontë's description of the Great Exhibition was written during a visit to London in a letter to her father, the Reverend Patrick Brontë. Dated May 31, 1851, the letter included an account of a lecture she attended by the novelist William Makepeace Thackeray, and a visit to the Great Exhibition in the Crystal Palace. Charlotte Brontë, *The Letters of Charlotte Brontë: With a Selection of Letters by Family and Friends: Volume Two, 1848–1851*, Oxford University Press, Oxford 2000.

[3] Fiona MacCarthy, *The Last Pre-Raphaelite: Edward Burne-Jones and the Victorian Imagination*, Faber and Faber, London 2011, p. 33.

[4] Celina Fox, *The Arts of Industry in the Age of Enlightenment*, Yale University Press, New Haven, Connecticut 2009, p. 453.

[5] Roland Barthes, "The New Citroën," in Roland Barthes, *Mythologies* Paladin, Frogmore, St. Albans 1973, p. 88–90.

[6] Richard Morphet (ed.), *Richard Hamilton*, exh. cat., Tate Gallery Publications, London 1992, p. 164.

[7] Sōetsu Yanagi, *The Unknown Craftsman: A Japanese Insight into Beauty*, Kodansha International, Tokyo 1972.

[8] Ana Elena Mallet, "Art in Daily Life: An Exhibition of Well-Designed Objects Made in Mexico, 1952," in Alejandra de la Paz, Virginia Ruano (eds.), *Clara Porset's Design: Creating a Modern Mexico*, Museo Franz Mayer, Mexico City, 2006, p. 45–56.

[9] John Neuhart, Marilyn Neuhart, Ray Eames, *Eames Design: The Work of the Office of Charles and Ray Eames*, Thames and Hudson, London 1989, p. 232–233.

[10] Richard Sennett, *The Craftsman*, Allen Lane, London 2008.

CHAPTER 4
The Descent of Objects

Renault=Présent, the 2016 book edited and designed by Irma Boom on a new Renault concept car, is printed on gleaming slithers of aluminum. This book was published in 2016 by Renault Design/ Laurens van den Acker.

The essence of an object has something to do with the way it turns into trash.
—*Roland Barthes*[1]

The audience laughed expectantly when Steve Jobs pointed toward the little rectangular pocket tucked inside the front right pocket of his jeans and asked: "Ever wondered what this pocket is for?" Apple's cofounder and CEO was speaking on September 7, 2005, at a launch event in San Francisco for its new products, and had already teased the crowd by promising to reveal "something pretty bold." A camera zoomed in toward the tiny pocket so the audience could see whatever he was about to pull out. "It's breathtaking," Jobs promised. "You won't believe it until you hold it in your hands … It is one of the most amazing products Apple has ever created."[2]

Jobs had been similarly hyperbolic when unveiling new Apple products

in the past, and would be again in future, but he professed
to be particularly proud of this one, the iPod Nano portable
music player. Yet less than 12 years later on July 27, 2017,
Apple announced that it was ceasing production of both the
once "breathtaking" iPod Nano and another former best-
seller, the iPod Shuffle. The decline in their sales had proved
so relentless that the company could no longer justify
manufacturing them.

Objects have come and gone from daily life throughout
history, after being supplanted by things that are—or seem
to be—superior in terms of their size, power, speed, durability, sustainability, or whatever else appeared more desirable
in design's equivalent of the Darwinian process of natural
selection. But there have been few eras in which so much
new stuff has appeared and so many old things have disap-
peared at such a frenzied pace as this one. Important though
it is to reflect on what innovations like robotic baby cribs,
quantum cryptography, and deep learning software will mean
to us in the future, it is also worth considering which of the
once ubiquitous objects that have long defined the design
of our physical surroundings we are likely to lose, and why.

The last time that the contents of daily life changed on a
similar scale was at the turn of the 20th century when the
introduction of electricity to millions of homes generated
the development of cleaner, more efficient electrical gizmos
that dispensed with the need for antiquated contraption,
such as gas lights. So thrilling did electricification seem at
the time that the Parisian artists Robert and Sonia Delaunay
took to arranging to meet their friends in places where
newly installed electric street lighting was to be switched
on, and to cheering loudly at the first glow of the bulbs.

The catalyst for the current changeover is the transistor,
the tiny device that conducts and amplifies power in
computers and other digital devices. Scientists have proved
so successful in their efforts to make transistors ever smaller
and more powerful since their invention in the late 1940s
that several million of them can now be packed onto a
microchip, which would originally have contained three or
four. As a result, our phones and computers have become

progressively smaller, lighter, and faster with such cavernous memories that they are able to fulfill the functions of
hundreds of different products: from printed books, newspapers, magazines, diaries, and maps, to telephone kiosks,
cameras, calculators, watches, Rolodexes, sound systems,
television sets, and the multiplicity of other things that
(depending on your viewpoint) either already are or soon
may be surplus to requirements, like those iPods.

Any object whose function can be executed more efficiently
by a digital application now faces the threat of extinction.
Take the door key. Exquisitely crafted though keys were
for centuries, and despite their rich symbolism—the word
"key" is, after all, a synonym for importance—how can a
jagged scrap of metal hope to compete against a smart lock
app that can open and close the doors of your home even
when you are not there? It cannot. The app is also safer.
Anyone can let themselves into a building or drive off in a
car if they find the key, but you can prevent them from
doing so with an app by protecting it with a security code,
which can, of course, be deleted if it is ever hacked. As with
so many other possible victims of the digital cull, keys are
what could be called "promissory objects." Like money and
postage stamps, their value lies not in themselves, but in
what they promise to deliver, making them superfluous,
and therefore disposable, as soon as something else emerges
that enables us to access it more efficiently.

Yet even things that are just as effective as their digital
equivalents are vulnerable too. The pocket calculator is an
example. Strange though it seems now, when pocket-sized
calculators were introduced in the 1970s, they seemed
dazzlingly technocratic with a seductive whiff of the then-
inscrutable world of computing. So tempting did they
appear to one Soviet diplomat that he secretly bought a
Sinclair Executive calculator on an official visit to the West
in the thick of the Cold War, only for it to explode in his shirt
pocket. His colleagues suspected foul play by Western agents,
but the Executive's feeble batteries were to blame.[3] Nearly a
decade later, the German band Kraftwerk dedicated a track
on its 1981 album *Computer World* to the pocket calculator with
the lyrics: "I am adding and subtracting. I'm controlling and

composing. By pressing down a special key, it plays a little melody."[4] A calculating application on a phone is no faster or more accurate than a traditional calculator, but the phone can do umpteen other things too, thereby trumping the Krautrockers' favorite gizmo in terms of convenience and environmental responsibility. Why waste scarce resources on manufacturing a gadget, which is no longer needed to fulfill its original function? And why bother carrying one around with you, when it has nothing else to offer?

Nor are all endangered objects as ancient as keys, or even pocket calculators. A few years ago, the design and tech blogs were agog with excitement about Apple and Samsung's plans to launch smartwatches. Both companies cheerfully predicted that those new gizmos would soon become ubiquitous. Their optimism diminished when people discovered that their expensive new watches could do little more than their smart phones. Moreover, those same phones had proved remarkably efficient at dissuading a generation of young consumers from wanting to wear wristwatches, smart or otherwise. Google encountered the same problem with what it once billed as the "next big thing," the ill-fated Google Glass that now seems as redundant as the PalmPilot personal digital assistants, which were so popular in their 1990s heyday.

Can other imperiled objects avoid the same fate? Only if there are special reasons to reprieve them. Take cameras. Most of them are doomed: especially those whose photographs are of similar or lower quality to phone snaps. But there are enough people who are more ambitious about photography and are willing to invest in sophisticated equipment to justify the continued production of high-quality cameras and to encourage their manufacturers to sustain their investment in the research and development required for those products to evolve. As a result, high-specification cameras have retained their functional edge over apps, whereas it is difficult to imagine pocket calculators, printed newspapers, or, even, keys doing the same.

Another possibility is for a product to be so beguiling in terms of how it looks or feels, and the associations it evokes, that it remains irresistible in its traditional form. Beautiful books made from exquisitely textured paper with visually compelling covers and typography fall into this category. They may have lost the struggle for the "survival of the fittest" against digital books—which are indisputably superior in terms of convenience, choice, connectivity, and ecological impact—but they could yet win another Darwinian battle, the one described in his 1871 book *The Descent of Man*. In that book, Darwin analyzes why some animals have physical features, which have no discernible practical purpose and appear to be purely aesthetic, seemingly disproving his earlier theory of natural selection. Yet such characteristics do have designated functions, or so Darwin explained, typically to arouse the desire of prospective mates, thereby persuading them to breed and propagate their species, as the peacock's magnificent tail and the richly colored plumage of male pheasants are intended to do.

A similar principle can be applied to otherwise obsolete objects. If they are desirable enough, they might survive, though not necessarily indefinitely. Conscious though I am of the functional shortcomings of printed books, I feel an affection for them, just as I do for finely crafted wristwatches, prompted by my memories of growing up with those objects. If I were in my teens or 20s, I would see them very differently, unencumbered by nostalgia, which is why, over time, fewer people will perceive them as being alluring.

There is also a risk that surviving in the fetishized form of beautifully fabricated artifacts made in expensive limited editions, as vinyl records have done, may prove to be a pyrrhic victory. Enticing though they can be, how can such elitist products recapture the cultural urgency that was so important an element of their predecessors' emotional appeal? Just as it is impossible to imagine a contemporary vinyl album cover articulating the spirit of a generation of young women as adroitly as Robert Mapplethorpe's 1975 portrait of an icily androgynous Patti Smith did on *Horses*, how can the jacket of a special edition book represent the hopes and fears of a section of society as eloquently as Penguin's paperbacks when the German graphic designer Jan Tschichold was head of design at the British publishing house in the late 1940s, scouring the printing presses for typos, and exaggerating his foreign accent to pretend he did not understand what the printers were saying when they grumbled about him? Impossible. The only foolproof way for an endangered object to survive is for it to have been designed so ingeniously that it offers us something its digital challengers cannot match.

An example is a traditional book, whose physical qualities enhance not only the reader's emotional attachment to it as an object, but their understanding of its contents. The Dutch designer Irma Boom does this brilliantly, often using the tactile qualities of unusual paper and unorthodox ways of cutting the page edges to guide us deftly through the text, or to tantalize us. Both tactics are deployed with aplomb in *Weaving as Metaphor*, the 2006 book she produced on the work of the US textile designer Sheila Hicks. Boom covered the book in uncoated, roughly textured white paper, which ages when handled, acquiring a patina that reminds its owner of the pleasure of reading and rereading it over the years. She also ensured that the page edges were cut to look and feel as raggedy and unkempt as the selvages of Hicks' textiles.[5] Boom described her design of *Weaving as Metaphor* as "A kind of manifesto for BOOKS. It makes the case for printed books over Internet, and proves that the book object can never be replaced."[6] She has since unveiled a succession of equally original, provocative, and intriguing books, including *Renault = Présent*, a corporate commission from Renault in 2016 to mark the launch of an electric concept car. The text and images are printed on gleaming slithers of aluminum that are as alluring to look at as they are to touch.[7]

Another Dutch designer, Joost Grootens has achieved a similar feat in reinventing the traditional printed atlas by devising new ways of organizing and depicting the information in the form of maps, charts, graphs, and other visualization techniques, which are best deciphered in print, not pixels.[8] As well as presenting new perspectives on geography and geology, his atlases deconstruct complex political conflicts, including a meticulous analysis of over a century of territorial battles between Israel and Palestine.[9] At a time when so many people have forsaken printed atlases in favor of satellite navigation and digital mapping, Grootens demonstrates how they can still be useful, as he has for another seemingly antiquated typology, the printed dictionary. In 2015, a new edition of the oldest and largest dictionary of the Dutch language, the Dikke Van Dale, was published after its traditional design template had been radically revised by Grootens. He ensured that the Dikke Van Dale's 5,000-plus pages were both more illuminating and easier to navigate by adding color coding, visual symbols, and illustrations, which gently nudge the readers to note useful references and associations that would elude a digital dictionary.

But Boom's and Grootens' books are rare exceptions. Unless other imperiled objects can produce equally convincing reasons to justify their continuation, they will be doomed to defeat in design's equivalent of the biological struggle for survival described by Charles Darwin in *The Descent of Man*— the descent of objects.

[1] Roland Barthes, "Non Multa Sed Multum," in Yvon Lambert (ed.), *Cy Twombly. Catalogue raisonné des oeuvres sur papier. Vol. VI 1973–1966*, Multhipla Edizioni, Milan 1976.

[2] "Apple Music Special Event 2005—The iPod Nano Introduction," uploaded by JoshuaG on February 13, 2006, https://www.youtube.com/watch?v=7GRv-kv5XEg.

[3] Nathan Ingraham, "An Ode to the Pocket Calculator, One of the First Mobile Computing Devices," *The Verge*, March 8, 2012, https://www.theverge.com/2012/3/8/2854488/pocket-calculator-mobile-computing-casualties.

[4] Kraftwerk's single *Pocket Calculator*, cowritten by Karl Bartos, Ralf Hütter, and Emil Schult, was released in 1981 having been recorded in seven different languages. It appeared on the band's 1981 album *Computer World*.

[5] Nina Stritzler-Levine (ed.), *Sheila Hicks: Weaving as Metaphor*, Yale University Press, New Haven, Connecticut 2006.

[6] Irma Boom (ed.), *Irma Boom: The Architecture of the Book, Books in Reverse Chronological Order 2013–1996*, Lecturis, Eindhoven 2013, p. 161.

[7] Irma Boom (ed.) *Renault = Présent*, Renault, Boulogne-Billancourt 2016.

[8] Joost Grootens, *I Swear I Use No Art at All: 10 Years, 100 Books, 18,788 Pages of Book Design*, 010 Publishers, Rotterdam 2010.

[9] Malkit Shoshan, *Atlas of the Conflict: Israel—Palestine*, 010 Publishers, Amsterdam 2013.

CHAPTER 5
Back to the Future

Originally designed by Norm Cox for a 1981 Xerox computer, the hamburger icon was revived by
Loren Brichter in 2008 to save screen space by symbolizing a website menu.

Everything should come from somewhere and go somewhere. The most important thing is obviousness. The problem is over design.
—*Loren Brichter*[1]

If you log on to one of the bigger, busier websites, like *The New York Times* or *The Guardian*, you may well spot three horizontal lines of equal length forming a small square at the top of the screen. It is known as the "hamburger icon," even though it is rather a stretch to read the upper and lower lines as the two halves of a bun, and the middle one as the meat, cheese, and whatever else is stuffed between them. Oddly named or not, those three lines have appeared on more and more websites in recent years, mostly to identify a menu that appears from the side of the screen to reveal a list of the contents.

Like all of the operating symbols on the screens of our laptops,

tablets, phones, and other digital devices, the hamburger
assumed its current function because something had to.
In its case, once smartphones had become powerful enough
to be used as internet browsers, website designers needed
to find ways of removing data from their pages to make them
easier to read on smaller screens. Replacing lengthy menus
with hidden ones that slid into view when you clicked on an
icon was a clever solution. The "side navigation panel," as
it is properly known, was devised in 2008 by the US software
designer Loren Brichter, who chose to identify it by reviving
the hamburger, which originally belonged to a pioneering
1980s digital user interface.[2]

Smart choice. Forget the sketchy resemblance to an actual
burger, those three lines look much more like extreme
abstractions of the chapter titles in a book index. The
allusion is apt, because a printed index fulfills much the
same function as a website menu. The hamburger is visually
appealing too, not least because it is ineluctably digital,
making it surprisingly rare amid the timid, often nostalgic
aesthetics of user interfaces.

Not that digital user interface design is a flop: in many
respects it is a triumph. Enabling billions of people to
operate something as brain-achingly complex as a computer
is a Herculean design challenge, which has become ever
more difficult as digital devices have shrunk in size while
increasing in power. The most important aspect of an
interface, or any other design project, is that it should fulfill
its function efficiently, but the experience of using it
matters too. Many of the most pleasurable aspects of
operating digital devices involve touch and movement, like
the "Pull-to-refresh" manoeuver with which we update our
email inboxes and Instagram feeds by tugging the top of the
screen. ("Pull-to-refresh" is another of Brichter's innovations.) But the visual dimension of user interfaces has been
less beguiling, even though digital operating symbols, like
the hamburger icon and the email apps on touchscreens, are
among the most ubiquitous images of our age, and our most
useful tools. Why are the aesthetics of something so perva-
sive, whose design is deeply sophisticated in other respects,
so often underwhelming?

When the first computers emerged in the 1950s, they were operated by specially trained technicians who typed instructions into typewriter-style keyboards in the form of programming code. Those machines were so big, and generated so much heat and noise, that most were placed in specially designated rooms. They were also so expensive that only very wealthy organizations could afford them. Not until the late 1970s did hobbyists—such as Apple's cofounders Steve Jobs and Steve Wozniak in the United States and Clive Sinclair in the United Kingdom—develop computer kits, which were small and cheap enough to be bought by individuals. The designers and programmers of the new personal computers then had to devise ways of enabling people who were unfamiliar with coding (the vast majority of their prospective customers) to operate them. Much of the early research into the design of digital interfaces—including Muriel Cooper's and Ron MacNeil's work in the Visible Language Workshop at the Massachusetts Institute of Technology from its inception in 1974 until Cooper's death in 1994—pursued that objective, while seeking to imbue digital imagery with the clarity and sensitivity of the best design in any medium.

The tech designer Bill Moggridge's 2007 book *Designing Interactions* describes how the first digital user interfaces were developed by computer scientists and design engineers in research laboratories, like the Xerox Palo Alto Research Center (Xerox PARC for short) in northern California. Their work was guided by the shared assumption that the closer a computer's controls appeared to be to familiar things with similar functions, the easier it would be to use them. To this end, they modeled the first digital user interface, which was introduced in 1981 with the Xerox 8010 "Star" computer on the flow of paperwork around an office—storing documents in files, folders, and cabinets, and discarding trash in bins—by creating pictorial replicas of those objects to represent the relevant controls.[3] The Star's interface featured several operating symbols created by a Xerox PARC design engineer, Norm Cox, including an empty rectangle that signified an A4 paper document and the hamburger icon.

Microsoft, Apple, and other companies adopted the office template too, while devising their own operating symbols to add to Xerox's. One Apple designer, Bill Atkinson, told Moggridge that during the development of the Lisa desktop computer in the early 1980s, they decided to warn its users when the trashcan needed to be emptied. Atkinson suggested that flies should buzz around the top, as they might in real life, only to be overruled by his colleagues. Worried that agitated insects would be too unsettling, they insisted on using crumpled sheets of white paper instead.[4] The Lisa sold poorly, but the trashcan's clinically pristine contents have outlived it.

Graphically, those early user interface symbols were fairly crude, not least because the pixels, from which digital images are constructed, were so big at the time. But, as computer graphics became more refined—with ever tinier pixels and subtler detailing—so did the quality of user interface imagery. In the last decade, we have become accustomed to seeing increasingly intricate operating symbols on the screens of our computers, smart phones, and tablets, many of them embellished by ornamental effects, such as drop shadows and *faux* textured or polished surfaces.

In theory, these advances should have empowered designers to create a singular new aesthetic, the early 21st century equivalent of the deftly designed controls of Braun electronic products in the 1950s and 1960s. Praising the glacial beauty of Braun's vintage radios and record players has become a design cliché, yet they remain models of the efficiency and elegance that Muriel Cooper sought for digital graphics. Braun's designers achieved this by minimizing the number of buttons, switches, and dials, positioning them in orderly sequences, and guiding the user with visual prompts like color coding. "Off" switches were always red, and "on" switches green. They even modified the shapes of the button tops to indicate whether they should be pushed down firmly or pressed at particular points: concave for the former, and convex for the latter. This formula enabled the products to be operated effortlessly, while creating an innovative and distinctive design aesthetic that still defines the era.

Instead of striving to produce something equally compelling, digital user interface design has been steeped in nostalgia. For much of the past decade, it has been dominated by hyper-realistic or skeuomorphic images of the type of analogue objects that Xerox PARC's designers used as prompts over 30 years ago. Take the paper envelope with an antique red wax seal that identified the email application in one Android Samsung phone. (The only digital touch was the @ of an email address stamped into the wax.) In 2012, Apple unveiled the iOS 6 operating software for iPhones and iPads whose graphic symbols included a traditional telephone handset for the phone app, an envelope for email, lined paper for notes and a clock whose similarity to the official Swiss Railways Clock provoked a legal row. (Apple conceded defeat, and eventually struck a deal to acquire the rights to use it.[5]) Even cheesier was the tacky wooden bookcase that identified the digital book store.

Why would any company invest so much money and creative energy in developing digital books only to present them as being much the same as printed ones? Why not illustrate them in a way that spelt out their benefits: such as offering a wider choice of instantly accessible titles without imperiling the environment by squandering paper, ink, and the fossil fuel required to ship traditional books from printers, to warehouses, and into bookshops? The analogue symbols that had seemed reassuring to tech *ingénues* in the early days of digital interfaces had become patronizing. They also risked baffling younger users, who may never have owned a landline phone, or any of the other physical objects, which were being rendered redundant by the very apps they symbolized.

A few weeks before iOS 6's debut, Microsoft introduced the Windows 8 operating system with a very different aesthetic. Simpler in style and bereft of decorative flurries, it was dominated by solid blocks of color and spruce typography. "Flat design," as it was called, was also adopted by Google, Twitter, Facebook, Dropbox, Samsung, and, eventually Apple. The styling of Apple's subsequent operating systems has been cleaner and less fussy than that of iOS 6, but is still replete with analogue references. Take the iOS 11 software,

which was introduced in autumn 2017 after being billed
with Apple's customary bluster as: "A giant step for iPhone.
A monumental leap for iPad." Despite the hyperbole,
the clock, camera, envelope, and lined paper symbols all
survived. Thankfully, the bookcase is long gone, though only
to be replaced by an old-fashioned printed book. The lone
ray of hope was the revival of my favorite skeuomorphic
feature in Apple's early interfaces, the calculator keypad
inspired by the 1977 Braun ET44 pocket calculator. It was
supplanted by a dreary piece of flat design in several iOS
versions, but returned in iOS 11, albeit in a slightly duller
version. Apple has shed its skeuomorphic excesses, but has
neither fully embraced flatness, nor succeeded in developing
a convincing new aesthetic.

Sadly, Apple's interfaces are not the only dull examples of
flat design, which although cleaner and sprucer than skeuo
styling with a pleasingly purposeful spirit, can be as dour
as its name suggests. Nor is the flat aesthetic free from
nostalgia, influenced as it is by the postwar European genre
of modernism, epitomized by the Swiss Style of typography
championed by Max Bill and Adrian Frutiger.

Developing a definitive design aesthetic as Braun once did
is fiendishly difficult in any context, but especially so for
something as complex as a digital interface with its multi-
farious functions. Whereas Braun's designers could depend
on the "form ever follows function" principle of modernist
industrial design to provide physical clues as to how to
operate their products, the designers of digital devices
cannot do so. How could you guess what to do with a tiny,
inscrutable smartphone or tablet by looking at it? You could
not. Another obstacle is the need to design operating
systems, which, like road signs, must be easily understood
by people with dramatically different levels of technological
knowledge and experience, without irritating the experts,
or confusing *ingénues*.

Yet user interface designers also have significant advantages.
Their field is relatively new, which is often conducive to a
gutsy and experimental approach to design. It also combines
huge brands with immense research resources, like Apple,

Google, and Microsoft, with plentiful opportunities for
entrepreneurial, attitudinal designers, such as Brichter,
to operate independently, free from corporate politics and
pressure to compromise. Nor is the visual aspect of user
interface design encumbered by formal constraints. There is
no legislative pressure to use specified operating symbols,
or an industry-wide agreement that compels companies
to do so. In theory, user interface designers have been free
to invent their own aesthetic, and have had the inestimable
advantage of powerful leaps in technology to help them.

Will they make more of these opportunities in future?
There is no reason why not, especially as interface design
has already achieved so much functionally and haptically.
If digital interfaces become equally imposing from a visual
perspective, we will all benefit. What would you rather see
on your screen? The unexpectedly eloquent hamburger,
whose only nod to nostalgia is to the pioneering early age
of computing, or a bookcase that looks equally unappealing
whether physical or digital?

[1] Jessica E. Lessin, "High Priest of App Design, at Home
     in Philly," *The Wall Street Journal*, March 17, 2013,
     https://www.wsj.com/articles/SB10001424127887324392804
     57835873099087367o.
[2] The original hamburger icon was designed by Norm Cox,
     a design engineer at the Xerox PARC research and
     development facility in Palo Alto, Northern California,
     for the 1981 computer, the Xerox 8010, or "Star." Loren
     Brichter revived it as a symbol to identify lists on Tweetie,
     an app he designed while working for Apple in 2008.
     Tweetie was designed to enable iPad users to use Twitter.
     "A Brief History of the Hamburger Icon – Placeit Blog,"
     https://blog.placeit.net/history-of-the-hamburger-icon.
[3] Bill Moggridge, *Designing Interactions*, The MIT Press,
     Cambridge, Massachusetts 2007, p. 53–54.

[4] Bill Moggridge, *Designing Interactions*, p. 101.
[5] The Swiss Railways Clock was designed in 1944 by Hans
     Hilfiker, an engineer and employee of SBB, the Swiss
     railway network. The design was trademarked and the
     clock is installed in railway stations throughout
     Switzerland. SBB sued Apple for breach of copyright in
     2012, claiming that the user interface symbol for the iOS 6
     clock was based on the Swiss Railways Clock. Apple
     subsequently agreed terms with SBB to acquire the
     licensing rights to the design. "Apple gets OK to use Swiss
     railway clock design," http://www.reuters.com/article/
     us-apple-iphone-swissclock-idUSBRE89B0SV20121012.

CHAPTER 6
Is Design Still a (Cis)Man's World?

Hella Jongerius (top) working in her Berlin studio with Edith van Berkel on an industrial design program for the Dutch national airline, KLM.

When I hear of other black designers I'm happy that they're out
there, just doing good work like
everyone else. I actually think the
women thing is a tougher nut to
crack. Ultimately, being a white
man is probably still the easiest.
There's no "Hey look, there's a … "
— *Gail Anderson*[1]

When Gertrud Arndt quit her job
in an architect's office in 1923 to
take up a scholarship at an art and
design school whose prospectus
promised to welcome "any person
of good repute, without regard to
age or sex," she had high hopes
of studying architecture. Instead,
she was urged to join the weaving
workshop, as were most of the
other women that enrolled as students at the Bauhaus. Those who
refused were encouraged to choose
ceramics on the grounds that it too
was suitably "feminine."

Nor was the Bauhaus alone in
perpetuating gender stereotypes.

A few years after Arndt's arrival, a young French interior designer Charlotte Perriand asked Le Corbusier for a job in his Parisian architectural studio only to be rebuffed with a curt: "We don't embroider cushions here."[2] Decades later, the viewers of a 1956 episode of the US television show *Home* watched a mortified Ray Eames join her husband Charles on air after being introduced by the (female) presenter with: "This is Mrs. Eames and she is going to tell us how she helps Charles design these chairs."[3] Another of Le Corbusier's collaborators, the British architect Jane Drew, who practiced with her husband Maxwell Fry, became so irritated by repeatedly being introduced as "Mrs Fry" at lectures, that she took to saying: "I'm sorry Mrs Fry can't be with us tonight, instead Miss Jane Drew has kindly accepted to replace her."[4]

No wonder that so many design history books are stuffed with references to men—mostly white men, though that is another story. Things have improved. A number of women designers are now recognized as being among the leaders in their fields: including Hella Jongerius in industrial design; Irma Boom in books; Ilse Crawford in interiors; and Hilary Cottam in social design. Other women have bagged the prestigious design prizes, professorships, and curatorships that once seemed to be reserved for men. Yet the most visible and commercially successful designers are still overwhelmingly male, even though female students have been in the majority at most North American and European design schools for more than two decades. And I have yet to meet a woman designer, successful or otherwise, who has not suffered from similar misogynistic slights and impediments to those that beset Arndt, Perriand, Eames, and Drew all those years ago. As for the rapidly expanding community of genderqueer designers who prefer not to identify themselves in traditional terms as cis male or cis female, they suffer from as much, if not more, prejudice.

Not that either group would be spared such obstacles in other fields, but they have had—and continue to have—an unusually tough time in design. Nor are they only victims of design's gender bias. The rest of us suffer too. If you believe that design plays an important part in organizing our lives

and in defining the objects, imagery, technologies, and spaces
that fill them, it stands to reason that we need designers
of the highest caliber. But we will not get them unless they
come from every area of society, not just from one gender.
Why has design remained a "man's world" for so long?
And how much longer will the gender politics of a discipline
that should, in theory, be open and eclectic, remain so
archaic given the surge of interest in fourth wave feminism,
transgenderism, and gender fluidity?

Women have, of course, practiced design throughout history,
albeit in the unconscious roles of "accidental designers,"
who produced doughtier tools or deadlier weapons on the
"necessity is the mother of invention" principle of instinctive
design ingenuity. Their work was rarely acknowledged,
though nor was that of the men who designed on the same
intuitive basis. Until the 20th century, only a tiny number
of women were permitted to work as professional designers,
and even they would have been unlikely to have done
so without the benefit of wealth and social connections.

Take Lady Elizabeth Templetown, the most successful of
the London socialites who persuaded Josiah Wedgwood to
allow them to decorate his pots during the late 1700s, when
dabbling in ceramic design was regarded as a fashionable
feminine accomplishment together with playing the piano
and needlepoint. Templetown was a star of the society
pages, and Wedgwood may well have been swayed by her
promotional value as much as her design skills, but some of
her patterns, mostly sentimental domestic scenes, became
bestsellers. Equally privileged were the cousins Agnes and
Rhoda Garrett, who claimed to be London's first female "art
decorators," or interior designers, a century later. Talented
and determined though they were, the Garretts were helped
by the financial support of Agnes' father, a prosperous
corn merchant, and by commissions from her sisters, who
included the women's suffrage campaigner Millicent Fawcett
and the pioneering doctor Elizabeth Garrett Anderson.[5]
Just as well, given that the sole architect they could persuade
to take them on as apprentices only agreed on condition
that they had nothing to do with the dirty, "unladylike"
construction process.[6]

Similarly, the first women to fulfill their architectural ambitions were mostly able to do so by building on their own land using their own money, as the British aristocrats Lady Elizabeth Wilbraham and Lady Anne Clifford did on their families' estates in the 17th century. Sarah Losh, the heiress to a Cumbrian industrial fortune, designed a church, school, and housing to be constructed on her property in the village of Wreay during the mid-1800s,[7] much as George Eliot's protagonist Dorothea Brooke hoped to do with her plan to build "good cottages" for her uncle's tenants in the 1874 novel *Middlemarch*. Even in the 20th century, as gifted a designer and architect as Eileen Gray struggled to secure commissions and was forced to name the design gallery she ran in Paris during the 1920s after an imaginary man, Jean Désert. Gray was only able to sustain her architectural career thanks to the private income that financed the construction of the houses she designed for herself. Charlotte Perriand was a rare exception in being one of the very few women from humble origins—her father worked as a tailor and her mother as a dressmaker in the Paris fashion industry—to succeed in establishing herself as a designer, and later an architect.

Yet even Perriand owed her success partly to male patronage, thanks to her relationship with Le Corbusier's cousin and chief collaborator, the Swiss architect Pierre Jeanneret. The same can be said of other prominent female designers of the early and mid-20th century, who were the wives or lovers of more famous male practitioners: as Marion Dorn was to Edward McKnight Kauffer, Lilly Reich to Mies van der Rohe, Jane Drew to Maxwell Fry, and Ray to Charles Eames. Often their achievements were confused with their partner's, or attributed to nepotism—and frequently both. So few women were employed as designers in the United States during the late-1950s that when Harley Earl, the head of design at General Motors, hired nine females to work alongside the scores of men in the company's design team, their presence was deemed so unusual that they were given a special name: the "Damsels of Design."[8] No one would have dreamt of giving male designers a nickname. Why bother, when they were ubiquitous?

Earl's motivation was pragmatic, not political. By then, two
out of every five drivers in the United States were female,
and GM's researchers had noted that they were far from
happy with the styling and functionality of their cars, which
were, of course, designed by, and for men. Decades later,
feminist design theorists, like the graphic designer Sheila
Levrant de Bretteville and her collaborators at the Women's
Graphics Center in Los Angeles,[9] were still deploring the
"gendering" of objects and images by the men who continued to commission most commercial design projects and
to dominate the design teams that developed them, imbuing
the results with their own values and ignoring women's
needs, or fobbing them off with clichés. Take the first
sneakers to be designed specifically for women, which were
introduced in the late 1970s and styled to reflect their
names, "Princess" and "Lady Jane," as opposed to "Revenge
Plus" and "Warrior" for the male equivalents.[10]

By the early 21st century, female designers were becoming
more numerous and, gradually, more influential. Not that
they have been spared the problems and prejudices faced by
women in other spheres: from sexist abuse and petty humilia-
tions, like being ignored by clients who insist on addressing
their male colleagues; to practical challenges, such as struggling to balance professional and personal responsibilities, or
discovering that a man with similar credentials is being paid
more for doing the same job. When the Australian conceptual
designer Gabriel A. Maher conducted an analysis in 2015 of
the depiction of gender in a year's issues of the Dutch design
magazine *Frame*, the findings were shocking. More than 80%
of the people—mostly designers and architects—photo-
graphed in the editorial pages and the models in the advertisements were presented as cis male. Typically they assumed
strong, powerful poses, and were described in heroic head-
lines such as "Master Meets Machine" and "Man with a
Purpose." The cis females adopted more submissive, sometimes coquettish guises, and were billed as "Design Divas,"
"Metal Matriarch," and other stereotypically derisory terms.
Later that year, IBM was forced to abandon a communica-
tions campaign intended to encourage women to work in
science, technology, and engineering design, after its target
audience expressed outrage at being "challenged" to "Hack

a Hairdryer." No wonder that teachers in design schools continue to report that even their most promising female students suffer from low self-esteem and other entitlement issues that have haunted women through the ages.

Yet there are more and more exceptions. Jongerius, Boom, Crawford, Cottam, and other accomplished female designers, such as Gail Anderson and Frith Kerr in graphics, act as inspiring role models for younger women. Some mixed gender design duos have chosen to work under the woman's name, rather than the man's; as Wieki Somers and her partner Dylan van den Berg do at Studio Wieki Somers in Rotterdam, and Patricia Urquiola does with Alberto Zontone in Milan. The accomplishments of once neglected female designers from the past are regularly celebrated in exhibitions, museum collections, and books. Many of the most influential design curators are female: notably Paola Antonelli at The Museum of Modern Art and Beatrice Galilee in New York; Zoë Ryan at the Art Institute of Chicago; Catherine Ince at the Victoria & Albert Museum in London; Matylda Krzykowski in Berlin; and Cecilia León de la Barra in Mexico City. At a time of growing interest in feminism, genderqueering, and the #MeToo and #TimesUp campaigns, the gender politics of design are explored in the books and debates organized by advocacy groups such as Hall of Femmes and the international Gender Design Network, both of which operate globally from their bases in Sweden and Germany, and in blogs like Depatriarchise Design run by the Zurich-based designer Maya Ober.

Even so, women still seem to struggle in established areas of design, in industrial design especially, possibly because a designer's prospects in those fields are determined by the mostly male powerbrokers that dispense prestigious commissions. Hella Jongerius is so far the only woman to have broken into the elite group of leading industrial designers and to have been commissioned to work on such ambitious projects as her KLM design program. Her work has already proved decisive in encouraging a greater emphasis on the nuances of texture, color, and symbolism in mass market products, and has been widely imitated, albeit generally with less rigor and sensitivity.

Gabriel A. Maher's research revealed that only 20% of the designers depicted in a year's issues of the design magazine *Frame*, from November 2012 to November 2013, were female-identified.

Tellingly, women tend to make more rapid progress in newer design disciplines, where there are no male gatekeepers to prevent them from assuming leadership roles, just as there were none to impede Muriel Cooper when she entered the fledgling field of digital design during the 1970s. Other women have since picked up her mantle, including the software designer Lisa Strausfeld, who was one of Cooper's students and named her daughter after her. Social design is another rapidly expanding area where women have thrived, including Bianca Elzenbaumer of Brave New Alps, Sara Khurram and Iffat Zafar of Sehat Kahani, and Emily Pilloton, who runs experimental courses to teach design and making as life skills in economically deprived communities in the US. Both Bilikiss Adebiyi-Abiola and Poonam Bir Kasturi[11] have developed influential sustainable design projects to improve waste management in Nigeria and India respectively. While Christien Meindertsma and the German designer Julia Lohmann are at the forefront of developments in conceptual design. They are following the lead of the British designer Fiona Raby, who did important early work in the field with her partner Anthony Dunne.

Given the speed of advances in science and technology, and the growing acceptance of the design process as a possible solution to an increasingly expansive range of economic, political, and environmental challenges, more new disciplines should surface in the future. Empowering though this will be for men, it should be even more so for women, by enabling them to operate independently in design, free from the constraints of old boys' networks.

Genderqueer designers should gain too. They stand to become prime beneficiaries of the new opportunities offered by attitudinal design, and should help to spare the rest of us from more of the misogynistic design solutions that so incensed feminist design theorists in the late 20th century. Incisive though such critiques were then, they seem less relevant at a time when interpretations of gender identity are becoming ever more nuanced, refined, and singular.

As binary definitions of cis male and cis female appear increasingly outdated, it is even more important for us to all be able to decide how to express the nuances of our personal identities in our design choices, rather than leaving it to the cis male establishment that has sustained the "man's world" of design for so long.

[1] Gail Anderson quoted in Alice Rawsthorn, "Design Gets More Diverse," *The International Herald Tribune*, March 21, 201,. www.nytimes.com/2011/03/21/arts/21iht-DESIGN21.html.

[2] Esther da Costa Meyer, "Simulated Domesticities: Perriand before Le Corbusier," in Mary McLeod (ed.), *Charlotte Perriand: An Art of Living*, Harry N. Abrams, New York 2003, p. 36–37.

[3] Charles and Ray Eames were interviewed on NBC's hour-long daytime magazine show *Home* in 1956 by its host and editor-in-chief, Arlene Francis. The 12-minute interview was timed to publicize the launch of the Eames Lounge Chair, designed by the Eameses for the US furniture manufacturer Herman Miller. "America Meets Charles and Ray Eames," posted by hermanmiller on November 23, 2011, https://www.youtube.com/watch?v=IBLMoMhlAfM.

[4] Shusha Guppy, "Obituary: Dame Jane Drew," *The Independent*, July 31, 1996, www.independent.co.uk/news/people/obituarydame-jane-drew-1307641.html.

[5] Elizabeth Crawford, *Enterprising Women: The Garretts and their Circle* (2002), Francis Boutle Publishers, London 2009.

[6] When Agnes and Rhoda Garrett exhibited their work in interior design at public exhibitions, the response was often hostile, sometimes blatantly misogynistic. One critic, Lewis F. Day, described their furniture they exhibited at the 1878 Paris World's Fair as "clumsy and tasteless." He also claimed that their installation was proof of "how little is enough to satisfy the ambition of lady-decorators." Annmarie Adams, *Architecture in the Family Way: Doctors, Houses and Women, 1870–1900*, McGill-Queen's University Press, Montreal and Kingston 2001, p. 151.

[7] Jenny Uglow, *The Pinecone: The Story of Sarah Losh, Forgotten Romantic Heroine – Antiquarian, Architect and Visionary*, Faber and Faber, London 2012, p. 198–199.

[8] General Motors' powerful head of design Harley Earl had hired Helene Rother as the company's first female designer in 1943 to help to choose colors and fabrics for car interiors. A second woman, Amy Stanley, joined the design team two years later. It was not until the mid-1950s, when Earl recruited more women, mostly graduates of the Pratt Institute's industrial design program, that General Motors used their presence as a promotional tool. Most of the "damsels" focused on designing car interiors, although four of the new recruits were dispatched to a General Motors subsidiary, the domestic appliance company, Frigidaire, where they designed trade exhibitions, including a "Kitchen of Tomorrow." Regina Lee Blaszczyk, *The Color Revolution*, The MIT Press, Cambridge, Massachusetts 2012, p. 249.

[9] The US graphic designer, Sheila Levrant de Bretteville, opened the Women's Graphics Center as a specialist resource inside the Woman's Building, which she had cofounded in Los Angeles in 1973 with the artist Judy Chicago and the art historian Arlene Raven, as a publicly accessible cultural and education center for women.

[10] Christine Boydell, "Pump up the Power," in Pat Kirkham (ed.), *The Gendered Object*, Manchester University Press, Manchester 1996, p. 121–132.

[11] The Indian design entrepreneur Poonam Bir Kasturi, who studied at the National Institute of Design in India, founded Daily Dump, as a fun and accessible way of encouraging people to compost their waste, thereby alleviating the pressure on the public refuse system in Bangalore. As well as designing and distributing composting kits, Daily Dump trains people in composting and helps similar groups to establish themselves in other places.

CHAPTER 7
Design's Color Problem

The National Museum of African American History and Culture (NMAAHC), designed by David Adjaye as lead designer and Philip Freelon as lead architect, beside the Washington Monument on the National Mall in Washington DC.

What I always strive for in my work is to engage people. I think it was Amílcar Cabral, an African revolutionary, who once said, "You have to be able to speak in a way so even a child can understand you."
I contemplated that and decided you even have to draw in a way that a child can understand you, so you can reach a broad audience without losing the essence or meaning of your work. In regard to my work with the Black Panther Party, it wasn't that the art came through me or by me, but it was a collective interpretation and expression from our community.
—*Emory Douglas*[1]

"What is a Pig?" is printed above a grotesque image of a pig hobbling on a crutch with tears streaming down its snout, torn clothes, bandaged limbs, and mosquitoes buzzing around its wounds. The answer to the question is written below: "A low natured beast that has no regard for law, justice, or the rights of people; a creature that bites the hand that feeds it; a foul, depraved traducer, usually found masquerading as the victim of an unprovoked attack."

Battle Fatigue is one of hundreds of drawings made during the US civil rights struggle of the late 1960s and 1970s by the graphic designer Emory Douglas in his role as Revolutionary Artist and, later, Minister of Culture of the Black Panther Party. Depicting the courage of the victims of racist abuse and the authorities' brutality against them, Douglas' images were published in *The Black Panther* newspaper and on fly posters pasted around the party's base in Oakland, California. His distinctive graphic style, combining bold contours and colors in unflinchingly vicious or poignant imagery, created an instantly recognizable visual identity for the movement. *Battle Fatigue*, which he drew in December 1967, also coined a word that became synonymous with repressive policing worldwide, "pig."

Gifted though he was, Douglas discovered design by chance, after being arrested in his teens and sentenced to 15 months at a Youth Training School in Ontario, California. He was assigned to work in the print shop, which gave him a crash course in typography, layout, and illustration. Once released, he studied graphic design at San Francisco City College, which was at the heart of the student protest movement. Flinging himself into activism, Douglas joined the newly formed Black Panther Party in 1967 and offered to help out by designing the launch issue of its official newspaper. He worked on *The Black Panther* until it closed in 1980.

Douglas is not quite as well known as might be expected of so talented and prolific a designer, especially one with such a picaresque story. Yet he has not been forgotten. The Museum of Contemporary Art in Los Angeles presented a retro-spective of his work in 2007,[2] followed by the New Museum in New York in 2009.[3] Both exhibitions helped to establish his graphics for the Black Panthers not only as important elements of the party's "radical chic" visual identity, but as models of smart political branding. His work is now part of the design collection of the National Museum of African American History and Culture (NMAAHC) in Washington DC.

Even so, Emory Douglas cuts a singular figure among
the elite group of designers who have been deemed worthy
of such exhibitions in the United States and elsewhere,
for the deeply dispiriting reason that he is black. Design has
long been accused of being a "man's world," but "white
man's world" would be more accurate, because that is what
has been portrayed in most books, exhibitions, and other
orthodox accounts of design history.

There has been progress, thanks to the recent success of
designers of color such as the Burkinabé architect Diébédo
Francis Kéré, the African-American product designer
Stephen Burks, the Nigerian fashion designer Duro Olowu,
and the British architect David Adjaye, who was born in
Tanzania to Ghanaian parents. Yet design remains less
ethnically diverse than most other creative disciplines,
arguably even art, which has its own inclusivity problems.
A whopping 86% of US graphic designers identify themselves as Caucasian, according to the American Institute of
Graphic Arts, which is higher than the comparable figure
for the general population. The same disparity applies to
the student bodies of design schools in North America and
Europe, although the number of Asian designers and design
students has risen steadily in both places.

The consequences are dire. If design is to fulfill its potential
to improve our quality of life it needs to attract the most
talented practitioners, and to reflect the nuances, complexi-
ties, and sensitivities of every area of society. How can it do
so if it continues to be dominated by a particular demo-
graphic, and a privileged one at that? Adjaye's research into
Africa's architectural heritage has enriched design discourse
in general, not just his own projects, which include the
National Museum of African American History and Culture
and the expansion of the Studio Museum in Harlem.
The fashion designer Grace Wales Bonner has had a similar
impact on her field by drawing on her British-Jamaican
identity in her collections, while the work of the African-
American fashion designer and art director Virgil Abloh is
inspired by both his Ghanaian parentage and the politics of
the US civil rights struggle. Why are there not more publicly
prominent designers of color to share their perspectives?

Historically, there was a simple explanation: designers of color suffered from the same discrimination as their peers in other fields, whether it was institutional in the form of segregation in the United States, or the outcome of personal racism. Norma Merrick Sklarek became one of the first black women to be licensed to practice architecture in the United States after graduating in 1950, only to fail to find a firm that was willing to hire her. Eventually she joined the New York Department of Public Works. Similarly, when Charles Harrison, a star industrial design student at the School of the Art Institute of Chicago in the early 1950s, applied to join the design team of the retail group Sears, Roebuck, he was told that it had an unofficial ban on employing African-Americans. Harrison was taken on by one of his former professors, and worked at a succession of Chicago design consultancies, often on projects for Sears, until the company offered him a job in 1961, making him its first African-American executive. Harrison was swiftly promoted to become head of corporate design, and developed many of Sears' most successful products, until he retired in 1993.

Most other African-American designers of the 20th century worked within the black community. Some were part of the counterculture movement, like Douglas, but the majority were employed within the cottage industry of African-American design firms, which were commissioned by African-American clients that also engaged African-American accountants, lawyers, and so on. Sklarek and Harrison were unusual in infiltrating the mainstream.

By the early 21st century, dynamic black designers like Abloh, Adjaye, Bonner, Burks, Kéré, and Olowu, were thriving in the United States and elsewhere. Every designer of color that I have encountered has experienced racism of some sort, ranging from unlawful discrimination, to being mistaken for someone in a menial job. Tellingly, some of the men attributed those problems to their youth, whereas the women were more sensitive to them and unsure whether they were triggered by their ethnicity, gender, or both. Both genders also recalled having felt compelled to prove their merits by working harder than their white contemporaries, especially at the start of their careers. Again, the women were more susceptible to this, and to feeling the pressure to excel more acutely.

As for design schools, most of them attribute the dearth of black students to the shortage of successful role models, who would give ambitious teenagers the confidence that they too could forge productive careers in design. The sad irony is that the competitive nature of design practice makes it a relatively meritocratic field where success tends to be determined by talent, charisma, and hard work, unless, of course, prejudice intervenes, and denies them the chance to prove their worth.

Hopefully, these impediments will disappear, as more talented designers of color emerge. The efforts to celebrate black designers from earlier eras—like Douglas with his museum shows and Harrison, who became the first African-American recipient of a Lifetime Achievement National Design Award in 2008—should help too. So should the debates and symposia on design and diversity, and the work of professional bodies, such as the Organization of Black Designers and the American Institute of Graphic Arts Diversity and Inclusion initiative in the United States.

Design's diversity problems in Europe and North America may also be assuaged by broader changes in its cultural geopolitics. During the 20th century, the dominant cultural influence on design internationally was European modernism, which was hatched in Eastern and Central Europe during the early 1900s then exported all over the world in the 1930s and 1940s by *émigrés* fleeing political persecution.

A defining theme of European modernism was the application of new technologies and rationalist design principles to produce huge quantities of identical objects at consistent quality for relatively low prices. This approach to design favored standardization over diversity, and wealthy countries with substantial industrial infrastructures over emerging economies. Even when developing countries strove to modernize their design cultures, they tended to ask Western designers for guidance—as the Indian government did by commissioning Charles and Ray Eames' report in the late 1950s. Unlike the Eameses and Charlotte Perriand, who completed a similar exercise for the Japanese government during the early 1940s, many of those designers advised their clients to adopt Western models of industrialization.

One of my favourite examples of design's role in liberating, as well as modernising a nation's identity is the work of the landscape architect Roberto Burle Marx in 20th-century Brazil. Like most wealthy Brazilians, Burle Marx had grown up among the roses, tulips, and other European plants imported during the colonial era. Not until he visited the botanical gardens in Berlin while studying art there in the 1920s did he discover the beauty of the native Brazilian plants, trees, and grasses that his compatriots dismissed as weeds. Burle Marx devoted his career to cultivating indigenous species, many of which he brought back from botanical research expeditions into the rain forest. He planted them in the gardens and parks he designed in a luscious tropical modernist style, including the grounds of government ministries in Brazil's new political capital, Brasilia, and the joyous two-and-a-half mile boardwalk of Copacabana Beach in Rio de Janeiro.

The passion and optimism with which Burle Marx expressed his vision of Brazil was exceptional for the time. Yet technological advances are now eroding the economic benefits of standardization by making it faster, cheaper, and easier to undertake ambitious architectural and industrial projects in developed and developing economies alike, and, increasingly, to customise the outcomes. As this process accelerates, designers will be able to become more expressive in reflecting the subtleties of their cultural identities in their work, including ethnicity, just as they will with regard to gender.

The digital tools that are fuelling the growth of attitudinal design projects among independent designers and design-entrepreneurs in North America and Western Europe are doing the same in Africa, Latin America, and South Asia. Some designers in those regions have leapt to the forefront of rapidly developing technologies, such as the African Internet of Things medical innovations that include Arthur

Testing the Peek Retina mobile eye diagnostic device, which was developed in Kenya by Peek Vision, a group of doctors and designers.

Zang's Cardiopad heart monitor and the Peek Retina eye diagnostic device developed by Peek Vision. Equally ingenious are entrepreneurial design projects, like the Ghana Bamboo Bikes Initiative. Based in Kumasi in southern Ghana, it was founded in 2009 as a nonprofit social enterprise by Bernice Dapaah, a business studies graduate, who teamed up with a group of engineering students to design light, robust bicycles to be made from fast-growing, abundant bamboo. They have since trained several dozen people, mostly young women, who previously had difficulty finding employment, to make the bikes.[4]

African design culture should also be strengthened by the recent investment in mammoth infrastructure programs. Among them is the production of clean, renewable energy that favors the very places that were geographically disadvantaged during the industrial age by their extreme climates as much as a dearth of investment. Uruguay, Paraguay, and Costa Rica already source more than 90% of their electricity from wind, solar, and hydropower. Morocco has ambitious plans for its recently constructed solar power plants, as does South Africa. As well as promising to transform the economies of these countries by reducing their reliance on expensive imported fossil fuel energy and enabling them to generate new streams of income by exporting surplus energy, these projects should leave a legacy of design and engineering expertise that can be constructively applied in other fields.

All of these projects—large and small—should inspire African designers to develop ever more ingenious and ambitious ideas while encouraging their peers in other countries to be more perceptive and generous about fostering greater diversity and inclusivity within their own design communities. Not until that happens can the rest of us be confident that we are making the most of the available design talent.

[1] Interviews, "Emory Douglas As Told to Courtney
     Yoshimura," https://www.artforum.com/words/id=64411.
[2] *The Black Panther: The Revolutionary Art of Emory Douglas*
     exhibition was presented at The Museum of Contemporary
     Art in Los Angeles from October 21 2007 to February 24,
     2008.
[3] *Emory Douglas: Black Panther* was presented at the New
     Museum, New York, from July 22 to October 18, 2009.
[4] By promising to plant ten new bamboo trees for each one
     it used, the Ghana Bamboo Bike Initiative hopes to help
     to arrest deforestation and soil erosion in rural Ghana.
     ghanabamboobikes.org.

CHAPTER 8
The Fun of the Fair

This 1981 photograph of the founding members of the Memphis design group in Masanori Umeda's *Tawaraya* boxing ring-shaped conversation pit was published in design media worldwide.

I see around me a professional disease of taking everything too seriously. One of my secrets is to joke all the time.
—*Achille Castiglioni*

Scoffing delicious *maccheroni al pomodoro* at La Latteria. Perching on one of Enzo Mari's *panettone* concrete traffic bollards. Finding Achille Castiglioni's design studio looking more or less as he left it at Studio Museo Achille Castiglioni. Spotting the remnants of the 1960s design scheme for the subway system, and Franco Albini and Franca Helg's granite benches. There is so much to enjoy on a visit to Milan.

Except, that is, if you go there during the six days in April when several hundred thousand designers, manufacturers, retailers, curators, editors, and bloggers descend on the city for its annual furniture fair, the Salone del Mobile. Not that you will not be able to go to La Latteria or Castiglioni's studio then, but

they will be very, very crowded. So will your flights to and
from Milan, and your hotel, which will have doubled,
or possibly trebled its rates. And good luck finding a taxi
or empty subway seat, because the Salone is not only
responsible for the busiest week of the year in Milan, but
in the global design calendar too.

Is it not odd that a furniture fair should exert so much power
throughout design culture, not just in its chosen field? So far,
the Salone has managed to do so, not least because of the
dearth of competition. How much longer can it continue to
pull it off at a time when design practice and the public's
understanding of design are becoming increasingly nuanced,
and so many other design challenges—from reconstructing
dysfunctional social services, to shielding us from the dark
side of neurorobotics—are becoming more important
to designers, and the rest of us, than tables and chairs?

When the Salone was founded in 1961, Milan seemed the
perfect place to host a culturally ambitious furniture fair.
It was the commercial heart of the Italian furniture industry,
which had made a critical contribution to the country's
postwar economic recovery by commissioning talented
designers, many of whom had originally trained as architects
or artists, to meld the region's historic artisanal skills
with recent technological breakthroughs in thoughtfully
developed, visually seductive products.

Most of the 12,000 visitors to the first edition of the fair
were Italian, but more people flocked there from further
afield throughout the 1960s and 1970s to see the latest
innovations of Gae Aulenti, Cini Boeri, Castiglioni, Joe
Colombo, Mari, Alessandro Mendini, Ettore Sottsass, and
the other Milanese designers who had forged close rapports
with enterprising local manufacturers. At their best, these
partnerships—like Castiglioni's with Flos, and Mari's with
Danese—lasted for many years and produced models of
enlightened industrial design that were efficient, beguiling,
and expressive. In 1972, The Museum of Modern Art in
New York celebrated the Italian furniture industry's finesse
in combining commercial clout with cultural vitality in the
exhibition *Italy: The New Domestic Landscape*. Curated by

the Argentinian architect Emilio Ambasz, it mixed mass-manufactured products with conceptual projects realized by the *avant garde* Florentine architecture groups Archizoom and Superstudio, and other members of the emerging Radical Design movement.

Nearly a decade later during the 1981 fair, some two thousand people descended on the Arc '74 art gallery for the opening of an exhibition of furniture by Memphis, a new design group formed a few months earlier. Photographs of its vibrantly colored, flamboyantly shaped furniture with its cartoonish symbolism were published all over the world. So was a team portrait of Sottsass, the group's leader, lounging with his young collaborators in a "conversation pit" designed in the form of a boxing ring by the Japanese architect Masanori Umeda.

Memphis was a true Milanese endeavor. The designers were of different nationalities, but the project was hatched in Sottsass' apartment on via San Galdino, and the furniture was made by local fabricators. Yet Memphis was also a triumph of perception over reality. Conceptually, there was nothing new about it. Sottsass had experimented with elements of the same aesthetic when working with Mendini and other pioneers of Radical Design during the 1970s. Nor was Memphis a commercial success: few of the designs sold more than 50 pieces. But its influence was immense. By distilling the principles of Radical Design into a form that was appealing and accessible to the public, Memphis popularized postmodern design theory by swamping not only design journals, like *Domus*, which was then edited by Mendini with Sottsass as art director, but the mass media too. Copycat versions of the Memphis style soon appeared in bars, hotels, and shopping malls all over the world.

But by demonstrating the promotional power of the Salone so convincingly, Memphis unwittingly condemned it to a relentless quest for something equally sensationalistic. Nothing else has quite matched it, despite the best efforts of mediagenic pranksters like the French designer Philippe Starck, whose publicity stunts dominated the coverage of the fair during the 1980s. Another debut show came closer in 1993, when the Droog group unveiled a gentler, subtler approach to design in the work of Jurgen Bey, Tejo Remy, and other recently graduated Dutch designers, who treated furniture as a conceptual rather than a commercial medium. (Though one member of Droog, Marcel Wanders, tried to meld the two and to outshine Starck, by sporting a clownish red nose in photographs, and throwing a party during the 2005 Milan Fair at which his barely dressed girlfriend topped up the guests' glasses with Champagne, and fed him grapes while swinging upside down from his newly launched chandelier.)

Ambitious young designers from all over the world have since flocked to Milan every April hoping to kick-start their careers by exhibiting their work during the fair. I once saw a couple of Swiss students installing an impromptu show on a traffic island, and spotted a young Milanese lighting designer, Federico Angi, doing the same in the windows of his uncle's carpentry workshop.

Will the Salone have the same allure in future? It is still a commercial colossus with over a thousand booths packed into the cavernous halls of the Fiera Milano convention center in Rho, to the west of the city. Navigating the halls can be exhausting, as is struggling through Milan's congested streets to far-flung fringe events. So many of them turn out to be promotional stunts seemingly unrelated to furniture or design, that the Salone del Mobile has been nicknamed the Salone del Marketing. Yet something always makes the slog around Milan worthwhile, whether it is finding a compelling new product, or an intriguing exhibition like those staged by Atelier Clerici, organized by the curators Joseph Grima and Jan Boelen, under Tiepolo's frescoes in sumptuous Palazzo Clerici. Even so, the Salone does not have quite the same clout it once had.

Attendance rose fairly steadily until the late 2000s, when the global property market collapsed in the credit crunch. Artek, Cappellini, Cassina, Flos, Poltrona Frau, and other prominent European furniture manufacturers were subsequently sold to new owners. The number of visitors to the Salone itself fell from 348,452 in 2008 to 278,000 the following year, then slowly recovered, although it was not until 2017 that the total came close to that of 2008.[1] Yet the media presence in Milan continued to grow throughout the credit crunch, feeding the Salone del Marketing element of the fair, while redefining its role within the furniture industry, which increasingly uses it as a showcase for new ideas. If the response in Milan is positive, the prototypes are turned into fully developed products, many of which are sold at the imm cologne furniture fair in Germany the following January.

Designers often complain of manufacturers rushing unfinished prototypes into the Salone to generate media coverage, and complain again if, as is often the case, they are not put into production. Even if they are, the designers' royalties are often paltry: most manufacturers still refuse to pay more than the 3% industry standard rate dating back to Castiglioni's heyday. Very few designers can expect to make a robust income from royalties as Edward Barber and Jay Osgerby, Ronan and Erwan Bouroullec, Konstantin Grcic, Hella Jongerius, Jasper Morrison, Starck, and Patricia Urquiola do. The odds are even shorter on them parlaying their exposure at the Salone into ambitious industrial commissions, like Jongerius's aircraft cabins for KLM.

The Milan furniture fair has become one of those highly visible, yet increasingly ambiguous events—like the Hay Festival on the Welsh Borders, Art Basel in Miami Beach in Florida, and Coachella in California—that are sustained as much by their promotional prowess as by their significance within their original fields. (Books for Hay; contemporary art for Miami Beach; and music for Coachella.) The problem is that the Salone faces growing tension between its official role as a trade fair (-cum-branding *bacchanal*) and its unofficial one as a design forum.

Both roles were sustainable in the last century, when furniture—and chairs in particular—occupied more cultural space than other design disciplines, which explains why so many design museums are stuffed with them, and why chairs have commanded the highest prices at design auctions. There was a rationale for this. In an age when design innovation tended to focus on physical things, the chair was an eloquent medium through which to trace the changes in aesthetics, technology, demographics, politics, and other spheres that influenced most areas of design. Furniture's cultural status was also strengthened by its links to architecture. Historically, whenever architects engaged with design beyond their own field, the outcome was often a chair, which is doubtless why Walter Gropius, Le Corbusier, Mies van der Rohe, Hermann Muthesius, and the other architects responsible for much of the critical discourse on design in the first half of the 20th century were so preoccupied by them. (Even though many of those architects delegated most or all of the design of their furniture to colleagues, often to women, as Le Corbusier did to Charlotte Perriand and Mies to Lilly Reich.) So were the architects-turned-curators who produced pioneering design exhibitions and museum collections, like Philip Johnson at The Museum of Modern Art in New York. In this context, why should a furniture fair not have exerted a wider influence across design culture, especially one associated with such landmarks as the debuts of Memphis and Droog?

Equally helpful to the Salone's cause was the support of the burgeoning industry of interior design magazines and blogs, and the Home sections of newspapers, which depended on its exhibitors for much of their advertising revenue, giving them a vested interest in the fair's continued success. But by dominating the media's portrayal of design, the Salone has unintentionally reinforced the popular stereotype of design as a superficial, stylistic tool steeped in consumerism.

Not that it is alone in this. The "design-art" market of fairs, galleries, and auctions has done so too, also unintentionally. There has always been a discrepancy between the perceived cultural and commercial value of art, but the gulf is far wider in design, which is a smaller, less mature sector with fewer sophisticated and knowledgeable collectors. The market for 20th-century design is riddled with aberrations: from selling furniture and fixtures that have been removed from Le Corbusier's public buildings in the Indian cities of Chandigarh and Ahmedabad to unknowing—or uncaring—Western collectors; to the cruel irony of Jean Prouvé's emergence as the super-capitalists' favorite furniture designer, when he devoted his working life to designing for the masses. But the contemporary market is even more distorted and distorting, given that by "design," it usually means visually striking, outlandishly expensive, but often impractical furniture. No wonder that public perceptions of as complex a field as design are dominated by the media coverage of yet another improbably shaped chair setting a new record price at a "design-art" auction,

This is not a new problem. As long ago as 1967, the British design historian Reyner Banham inveighed against what he called "furniturization" in an essay for the political journal *New Society*. "The area worst blighted by furniturization lies right under the human arse," wrote Banham. "Check the area under yours at this moment. The chances are that it is occupied by an object too pompous for the function performed, over-elaborate for the performance actually delivered and uncomfortable anyhow."[2] Rampant though furniturization was then, it has become even more so since the Milan fair's post-Memphis metamorphosis as the Salone del Marketing, and the beginning of the "design-art" boom in the late 1990s.

Conversely, other areas of design have become increasingly attitudinal—diverse, ambitious, intellectually dynamic, and politically engaged. This shift is evident in the content of the most interesting student shows presented in empty factories and warehouses during the Milan fair. A decade ago, many students seemed set on following Wanders' example by positioning themselves as mini-Starcks; now they are likelier to aspire to making meaningful contributions to ecological catastrophes, or to redefining design's interpretation of gender identity. Why would they choose to devote their careers to producing more chairs and tables, when so many arguably more interesting and rewarding possibilities are open to them? The design landscape has changed so dramatically since Droog's debut, let alone Memphis', that it is impossible to imagine future developments in furniture having a similar cultural impact. Moreover, the furniture designers of the future are as likely to spend their time devising ways of enabling the rest of us to customize chairs on the next generation of 3D printers, as on developing those objects themselves.

Many of these new design challenges are explored in the fringe exhibitions held during the Salone del Mobile, like Atelier Clerici's shows and the menders' market assembled outside La Rinascente department store on Piazza del Duomo in 2014 by Martino Gamper to show off the restorative skills of local cobblers, bookbinders, 3D printers, and cycle repairers. But a furniture fair is not necessarily an empathic or effective forum for them, raising the possibility of their migrating elsewhere. Just as imm cologne has emerged as a robust commercial competitor to Milan, a number of small but feisty cultural events have become increasingly influential within design discourse, such as the Ljubljana and Istanbul design biennials, the Beijing and Vienna Design Weeks and the increasingly popular Dutch Design Week in Eindhoven. The furniture industry is experimenting with the cultural dimension of design too, notably in the architecture park of buildings designed by Herzog & de Meuron, SANAA, Alvaro Siza, Frank Gehry, and the late Zaha Hadid at Vitra's manufacturing base at Weil-am-Rhein on the Swiss-German border. Hundreds of thousands of "design tourists" visit the site each year to see the architecture and intriguing additions, including a Jean Prouvé gas station, one of Buckminster Fuller's geodesic domes, and a set of bus shelters designed by Jasper Morrison, as well as the exhibitions of furniture and other aspects of design presented at the Vitra Design Museum.

None of these endeavors commands as large an audience or as much media attention as Milan Design Week, nor has another city mounted a knockout bid to host the preeminent annual design fest, although Eindhoven stands a fighting chance of doing so if Dutch Design Week maintains its current momentum. Even so, there is now a wider choice of possibly more congenial homes for the polemical design projects that may not have been on the Salone del Mobile's official agenda, but that have given it so much prestige and vibrance over the years.

[1]   www.salonemilano.it/en/media/comunicati-stampa.html.
[2]   Reyner Banham, "Chairs as Art," *New Society*, April 20, 1967.

Some of the artisans and fixers assembled by the Italian designer Martino Gamper outside La Rinascente department store in Milan in April 2014 for the *In a State of Repair* project.

CHAPTER 9
Choices, Choices, Choices

The discreetly elegant Georg stool, devised by the Danish designer Chris Liljenberg Halstrøm for the Danish manufacturer Skagerak, is a design experiment in gender fluidity.

Beyond the age of information
comes the age of choices.
—*Charles Eames*[1]

When Aimee Mullins was 16, she
was given a new pair of lower legs.
Made from woven carbon fiber,
they were lighter and stronger than
the wood-plastic compound prostheses she had worn until then,
as well as being easier to put on,
less painful to wear, and less likely
to fall off. So far so good—except
that those legs were designed to
be worn by both men and women,
and were coated in a thick foam
that came in just two colours:
one named "Caucasian," the other
"Not Caucasian."

That was in 1992, and Mullins now
has many more legs to choose
from. Among them are four pairs of
silicon-covered prostheses, each
one specially designed to her specifications. One pair is fitted with flat
feet, and the other three with feet
shaped to fit shoes with two, three,

and four-inch heels respectively. Not that she will need them for much longer, as her newest legs are equipped with adjustable ankles. For hiking, Mullins wears carbon fiber Vertical Shock Pylon (VSP for short) limbs fitted with shock absorbers; and for swimming, she dons an old pair of VSPs with holes drilled into the sockets to allow water to drain through. These are just the prostheses she has to choose from at home in Los Angeles.[2] Other legs designed especially for her, including the transparent polyurethane ones she wore in Matthew Barney's 2002 film *CREMASTER 3*, are carefully conserved in archives.

Having so wide a choice of lower limbs has helped Mullins to build a career as an actor, model, athlete, and activist, but most of them only exist because of the time and energy she invested in their design, and in convincing the prosthetists, biomechatronic engineers, designers, cosmeticians, and artists with whom she has collaborated to do the same. Had Mullins accepted the standardized legs she was offered—which was her only option when presented with "Caucasian" or "Not Caucasian"—her life would have been very different. By immersing herself in the design process, Mullins instinctively fulfilled the role of an attitudinal designer, and secured her right to wider and better choices, empowering not only herself with her experiments, but millions of other people whose prostheses have subsequently been better designed to meet their needs and desires.

Choice will be a defining element of design in future. As our personal identities become subtler and more singular, we will wish to make increasingly complex and nuanced choices about the design of many aspects of our lives, just as Mullins has done. We will also have more of the technological tools required to do so. If design is to respond to our needs and wants, it must find new ways of delivering the choices we crave, even though this will demand radical shifts in design practice.

Up until now, many important design innovations have restricted choice, either in the way they were made or how they were used. Not that choice was deemed undesirable—quite the contrary—but it was often considered dispensable in the interests of other qualities such as efficiency, speed, economy, convenience, and inclusivity, which is why standardization has loomed so large in design history.

As long ago as the 3ʳᵈ century BC, a decisive factor in the success of Ying Zheng, the teenage king of the obscure Asian state, Qin, in defeating his richer, more powerful neighbors to found the mighty Chinese empire was the uniform design of his weaponry. At the time, weapons were made by hand to different specifications. Ying insisted that all of his army's spears, axes, daggers, and arrows were designed to identical templates, all devised to be as deadly as possible. Until then, if archers ran out of arrows, they could not fire their comrades' arrows from their bows. Ensuring that they were interchangeable solved this problem, and Ying's formidably efficient army won battle after battle.[3] Similar design principles were applied in the workshop of the French gunsmith Honoré Blanc in the late 18ᵗʰ century. When Thomas Jefferson visited Blanc there as a young US diplomat, he was so impressed that he submitted a report urging newly built factories in the United States to adopt the same system.[4]

Standardization was also deployed to more empathic ends. Take the cemeteries of the Shaker Villages built on the East Coast of the United States after Mother Ann Lee, the leader of the radical Quaker sect known as the United Society of Believers in Christ's Second Appearing, or Shakers, fled there with eight followers in 1774 to escape political and religious persecution in Britain. Fairness, equality, and humility were defining elements of Shaker culture, and were reflected in the design of the villages and their contents, most poignantly in the cemeteries, where each gravestone was identical in size and shape in the spirit of modesty and egalitarianism.

Outside the Shakers' self-sufficient enclaves, standardized design became a cornerstone of the Industrial Revolution. It was even applied on an artisanal scale by enterprising craftspeople, like David Kirkness, a carpenter in the Orkney Islands north of Scotland. He designed four versions of a chair, which resourceful islanders had made for centuries from pieces of driftwood and the straw left over from growing their staple crop, oats. The frames of all four chairs were designed for ease of production in his workshop, while the seats and backs were woven by fellow Orcadians, mostly working at night after finishing their day jobs. Kirkness sold over fourteen thousand of his Orkney Chairs, including one to the artist Augustus John.

By the early 20th century, management theorists, led by Frederick Winslow Taylor, were advocating the standardization of every aspect of manufacturing, starting with design.[5] Among Taylor's devotees was the Detroit motor manufacturer Henry Ford. Having discovered that the lengthiest part of Ford's production process was waiting for the paint to dry, he urged his sales force to push black cars, as black was the fastest drying color. His "pledge" that "any customer can have a car painted any color that he wants as long as it is black," became a slogan of the rigorously uniform Fordist model of mass-manufacturing, which was adopted worldwide during the 20th century, and reinforced by ever stricter health and safety regulations.

Not everyone was in favor. During the 1950s and 1960s, the films of the French director Jacques Tati parodied what he saw as the soullessness of standardization and globalization. For his 1967 film *Playtime*, Tati spent millions of francs on building a miniature city on the outskirts of Paris with two skyscrapers, a power plant and a stretch of road with working traffic lights. He showed his befuddled anti-hero Monsieur Hulot losing his way among the indistinguishable buildings. When Tativille, as the set was called, was damaged in a storm, he borrowed heavily to repair it, but the film flopped and the 70 year-old Tati was declared bankrupt.

Soulless though it could be, standardized design transformed billions of people's lives by offering them safer, more robust and reliable products and services. It even earned the modern movement's blessing for delivering "the best for the most for the least," as Charles Eames put it. Not everything was standardized. The rich continued to have things designed and made especially for them, and the poor had no alternative. But for much of the 20th century, idiosyncrasy was seen as a throwback to an impoverished, poorly educated preindustrial culture. By the beginning of this century, it was uniformity's turn to be demonized and associated with blandness at best, and, at worst, with labor exploitation and environmental destruction.

It is not difficult to understand why. Firstly, it is impossible to ignore the ugly truth about the human and ecological damage wrought by industrialization. Secondly, even the most basic forms of digital technology have enabled us to exercise greater choice: whether by navigating our own paths around the Internet to extract information from whichever websites take our fancy; determining the outcome of video games; or tszujing our personae on social media. Television talent and makeover shows have contributed too, by dangling the tantalizing prospect of transformation before us, as have cosmetic surgery ads.

These changes have encouraged us to expect greater choice in other aspects of our lives, and the politics of personal identity have metamorphosed. Take the media storm in the United States in 2015 over the revelation that Rachel Dolezal, a civil rights activist born to white parents, had chosen to present herself as black in a country where being biologically black is fraught with peril. Or the explosion of interest in transgenderism and genderqueer identities. When Facebook introduced more than 50 "gender options" with which its US users could choose to describe themselves in 2014, there was such a furious outcry that the company replaced them with a free-form field, which people are free to fill in as they wish. Given that our perceptions of ourselves seem set to become even more mercurial in future, design must adapt to help us to express them.

Some design disciplines have done so successfully for centuries, specifically those, like fashion and graphics, that can be customised easily and cheaply to articulate anything from personal preferences, to our political concerns. When Sylvia Pankhurst was charged with designing the visual identity of the British women's suffrage movement in the early 1900s, she was mindful that many working class members could not afford to buy badges or sashes.

Her solution was to choose a color-coded identity of white for purity, purple for dignity, and green for hope. Wealthy suffragettes purchased banners or hatpins in those colors to support the movement financially, while others could improvise by using scraps of fabric or ribbons in those hues. African-American civil rights campaigners deployed similar tactics in the 1960s by coding their appearance: from growing out their hair into natural afros, to wearing dashikis, the loose shirts made from richly patterned *kente* cloth that originated in West Africa. Each element was carefully chosen to declare that the wearer was refusing to conform to white stereotypes in favor of honoring their African heritage.

Other areas of design have proved more difficult to personalize, notably the industrial design programs that depend on uniformity to achieve the economies of scale required to manufacture digital devices or kitchen appliances on an affordable basis. Consider how these obstacles can be overcome in what is currently one of the most contentious aspects of personal identity: gender. One way of avoiding traditional stereotypes, such as "male" products being designed for taller, stronger people than "female" ones, is to develop objects as kits of parts that can be combined in different ways to suit their users. The French brothers Ronan and Erwan Bouroullec have devised ingenious examples in their modular seating, screens, offices, and kitchens that can acquire new functions and be made larger or smaller by adding or removing components. The Bouroullecs do not design with gender politics in mind, but the flexibility of their mass-manufactured products addresses that agenda tangentially.

Other designers are tackling gender issues directly, including the Danish-Swedish furniture designer Chris Liljenberg Halstrøm, who produces objects with a neutral aesthetic that is open to individual interpretation. Halstrøm's design process begins by visualizing how the product will be used, regardless of gender. Striking colors, shapes, symbols, and other visual cues are avoided as they are often loaded with clichés. Instead, Halstrøm uses texture to lend character to objects in the belief that our sense of touch is less likely to be gendered. The Georg stool, designed

by Halstrøm for the Danish furniture maker Skagerak,
consists of a pillow covered in richly textured fabric
strapped on to a wooden base. Each sitter can adjust
the pillow to suit themselves, and, in doing so, discover
the pleasure of touching the fabric.

Not that everyone will read Georg in that way. Halstrøm's
stool has won several mainstream design awards based on its
conventional merits as a robust, comfortable, and elegant
piece of furniture, rather than for subverting gender stereotypes. Nor is neutrality the only way of designing products
that permit more fluid and eclectic interpretations of
gender. An alternative approach is to reflect the multiplicity
of possible identities as the British designer Faye Toogood
did in 2015 by combining elements of a neutral aesthetic
with a diverse mix of colors, textures, and shapes in Agender,
a retail experiment conducted by Selfridge's to sell gender-
neutral fashion in its department stores in London,
Manchester, and Birmingham.

The Australian designer Gabriel A. Maher has applied a
similar approach in design research projects, which experiment with new typologies of clothing and furniture that
allow each individual to choose how to interpret them,
as well as challenging gender clichés. So have the Swedish
designers of the Toca Boca educational play apps for
children, by striving to avoid stereotypes and present a fluid
depiction of gender. The clients in the Toca Hair Salon
include cis male and cis female characters as well as a few
whose gender identity appears to be ambiguous. The same
applies to the scientists working in the Toca Lab, which
looks very different to a conventionally clinical laboratory,
with its vivid pastel colors and soft, fuzzy shapes. Even the
text describing the games is written in a liberating spirit.
Take the Toca Cars driving game description: "Buckle up,
friends! In Toca Cars you do what feels right. No rules apply
to these roads. Cruise through big puddles of ice cream,
fly off jumps into a lake or build a huge piles of houses, stop
lights, and mailboxes and drive right through … "

Future leaps in technology will enable us to exercise greater
choice in design by customizing objects and environments

ourselves. The chief catalyst will be the development of increasingly sophisticated and affordable digital fabrication systems, like 3D printing. The current crop of publicly accessible 3D printers are limited in terms of the size of objects and range of materials they can process, which may explain why they so often churn out ornamental knick-knacks. As the technology becomes more refined, it should be capable of making entire objects, or parts of them, so speedily and accurately that they can be produced individu-ally, and personalized in terms of their palettes, textures, finishes, and shapes. In doing so, they will fulfill the vision of "mass customization" championed by radical late 20th-century design theorists, such as the German activist Jochen Gros. *The Economist* has long predicted a future in which each local community will have a 3D printshop of its own where local people can make new personalized objects, and repair or adapt existing ones, just as their ancestors once did by handing them to a blacksmith at the village forge.[6] We should then be able to replace dented car doors with identical 3D printed ones, and to choose how the details of objects will reflect the dynamics of our gender identities, or any other attributes, as easily as we can with clothing.

Will we want to exercise this level of choice? It is easy to understand why Aimee Mullins should wish to design bespoke 3D printed prostheses, or why someone with arthritic hands might benefit from using a steering wheel that is easier to grip, but will other people be willing to invest as much effort in design? Some will not, just as not everyone wants to cook their own food or sew their own clothes. But the popularity of knitathons, makers' libraries, pottery classes, and "teach yourself to code" devices, like the tiny $25 Raspberry Pi programmable computer, and low-tech video game publishing programs such as Twine, suggests that others will. Twine is already enabling designers to explore deeply personal issues in their games, including gender identity, which is a defining theme of Porpentine's *All I Want Is For All Of My Friends To Become Insanely Powerful*[7] and Taylor Last's *Space Alleviator*.[8]

If more and more of us engage with design, where will this leave designers? Some will continue to work in the

The Toca Lab educational play app for children was designed by Toca Boca to quash gender stereotypes and to empower kids to choose freely.

traditional way, but others will redefine their roles to help us to make design decisions, rather than doing so on our behalf. Critically, they must also learn how to act as guides to the design process. In an age of seemingly limitless design choices, picking the right ones will be more important than ever.

[1] Carla Hartman, Eames Demetrios (eds.), *100 Quotes by Charles Eames*, Eames Office, Santa Monica, California 2007.

[2] Author's interview with Aimee Mullins, October 16, 2015. The US-born actor, model and athlete, Aimee Mullins (1976–) set three world records for the 100-meters, 200-meters, and long jump at the 1996 Paralympic Games in Atlanta, Georgia. Mullins is a bilateral amputee, who was born without fibulae in both legs, which were amputated below the knees on her first birthday. As a model, she worked closely with the late British fashion designer, Alexander McQueen. She also forged a close collaboration with the artist Matthew Barney, and acted in several of his films, including *Cremaster 3* (2002) and *River of Fundament* (2014). Mullins has appeared in feature films and TV series, including *Stranger Things* (2016 and 2017).

[3] Robin D.S. Yates, "The Rise of Qin and the Military Conquest of the Warring Sstates," in Jane Portal (ed.), *The First Emperor: China's Terracotta Army*, The British Museum Press, London 2007, p. 31.

[4] John Heskett, *Industrial Design*, Thames & Hudson, London 1980, p. 50.

[5] Frederick Winslow Taylor, *The Principles of Scientific Management* (1911), Dover Publications, Mineola, New York 2003.

[6] "Print me a Stradivarius," *The Economist*, February 12, 2011, www.economist.com/node/18114327.

[7] Laura Hudson, "Twine, the Video-Game Technology for All," *The New York Times Magazine*, November 19, 2014, https://www.nytimes.com/2014/11/23/magazine/twine-the-video-game-technology-for-all.html.

[8] https://raining.itch.io.

One of the Agender shops selling ungendered clothing and accessories. The shops were designed by Faye Toogood in 2015 for Selfridge's department stores in London, Birmingham, and Manchester.

CHAPTER 10
Out of Control

The Oost road junction in the Dutch town of Oosterwolde was converted by Hans Monderman into a shared street where drivers, cyclists, and pedestrians can mix together, negotiating their right of way by means of informal social rules rather than by defined traffic rules. Kerbs were removed so there is no clear physical demarcation between the pavement and the rest of the street. The theory of shared streets like this is that when people feel a situation is potentially unsafe, they stay alert, reduce their speed, and thereby cause fewer accidents.

I'm sorry Dave, I'm afraid I can't
do that.
—*HAL 9000*[1]

Baffling though it may seem
to anyone who suffers the delays,
overcrowded trains, broken lifts,
and other shortcomings of the
London Underground today, it was
once hailed as a model of modern
design. Under its visionary managing director Frank Pick, the
Underground not only introduced
its passengers to modernist architecture and graphics during the
early 20th century, but pioneered
mechanical innovations like electric
ticket machines, escalators, and
pneumatic train doors. The only
problem with those gizmos was
that many of the passengers were
too terrified to use them.

Pick and his colleagues were so
concerned that, in 1937, they
commissioned László Moholy-Nagy
to design posters explaining why
the new contraptions were not as

frightening as people seemed to fear. Having fled Nazi Germany for fear of oppression, Moholy-Nagy was reduced to scraping a living from commercial design jobs like this one as an émigré in London. One of his posters sported the soothing title *Soon in the Train by Escalator*, above an illustration of wooden escalator steps with cutaway images revealing what the machinery inside looked like when "beginning to go down" and "going down." A brief text described how it all worked.

Soon in the Train by Escalator fulfilled one of design's most important, yet often unsung roles: that of helping us to adjust to changes in the logistics of daily life by dispelling our fears. Another of Pick's inspired design commissions, Harry Beck's 1933 diagrammatic map of the London Underground, enabled bemused passengers to navigate the sprawling network more efficiently than they could have done with a geographical map. Similarly, Moholy-Nagy's poster encouraged them to believe that they might glide effortlessly up the escalator from the platform to the exit, rather than being doomed to panic about falling or getting tangled up in the machinery. Both designs gave people the confidence to cede control to a potentially daunting innovation by convincing them that they understood it.

Control remains a critically important element of design today, yet our relationship to it is changing radically. Many of the technologies we now use are so powerful and complex, and will become even more so in future, that any attempt to make us think we can control them would be pointless. In the age of neuromorphic and quantum computing, cryptocurrencies, blockchains, artificial intelligence, cloudification, smart cities, and other developments that promise to take charge of more and more aspects of our lives, the new design challenge is to ensure that it really will be in our best interests to be controlled by them, because they will change our lives for better not worse.

Achieving this will require a fundamental shift in design culture, because helping us to feel as though we are in control was the driving force of so many past design triumphs. Take the signage systems that enabled motorists

to drive swiftly and safely on newly built roads and motor-
ways, like those designed by Jock Kinneir and Margaret
Calvert in Britain during the late 1950s and 1960s,[2] and helped
airline passengers to navigate the labyrinthine layout of
newly opened airports.[3] Or the user interface software with
which people operate cars, record players, television sets,
computers, and smartphones. When designed intelligently,
they have empowered millions of us to conquer our fear
of the new. If their design was botched, the consequences
could be infuriating, as Jacques Tati's hapless Monsieur
Hulot discovers when visiting his brother's ultra-modern
house in the 1958 film *Mon Oncle*. One by one, the house's
futuristic gizmos malfunction, from the uncontrollable
electronic garage doors that open and close inexplicably,
to the inscrutable kitchen gadgets.

Often, designers have tried to reconcile us to new things
by suggesting that they are not so very different from
familiar ones by deploying skeuomorphic design references.
The wooden casing of the escalator in Moholy-Nagy's poster
served as an early example, by disguising those newfangled
mechanical stairs as traditional wooden ones. The same
rationale explains why we type instructions to computers
on old-fashioned Qwerty typewriter keyboards, and why
the applications on so many smartphone and tablet screens
are identified by images of the books, cameras, letters, and
other analogue objects that they are threatening to replace.

Designers now need to develop different strategies.
One problem is that we have become so adept at decoding
some of the old ones, that they are becoming less effective.
The fiery debate about skeuomorphism suggests that more
and more of us are so confident about using digital devices
that we not only consider such cues to be superfluous,
but feel patronized by seeing a paper envelope identifying
the email app and a telephone handset for the phone on
a supposedly state-of-the-art smartphone.

Our response to design strategies, which were once successful at helping us to deal with hazardous situations like driving
or cycling, is changing too. Why are there fewer accidents
on roads after the signs, white lines, speed bumps and other

"traffic calming" ploys have been removed? Is it because if motorists lose the illusion that a road is safe, they tend to slow down and become more vigilant? And why do more accidents in cities occur at traffic lights than anywhere else? One theory is that drivers and cyclists alike have grown so accustomed to them that they focus on the lights, not the traffic, and presume—not always correctly—that everyone else will follow the rules too.

Some of the most constructive responses to this problem originated in the work of the Dutch traffic engineer, Hans Monderman, during the 1980s and 1990s. Convinced that encouraging drivers to use common sense and intelligence would make roads safer than arsenals of signs, Monderman applied his experience as a civic engineer and accident investigator to design what he called "naked streets" and "shared spaces," bereft of controls. His experiments in the Netherlands succeeded in reducing speeding offences, congestion, and accidents, and have since been reinvented with similar results in the design of new "naked streets," such as Sonnenfelsplatz in the Austrian city of Graz, and Exhibition Road beside the Victoria & Albert Museum in London. (Confession: I am so bewildered by the dearth of controls on Exhibition Road that I drive up and down it much more cautiously than I would on a conventional street.)

Empowering individuals to reclaim control may be an efficient design strategy for road safety (if only for the time being), but not when it comes to encouraging us to engage with the latest wave of transformative technologies. Things which would have seemed like the stuff of fantasy only a decade ago are now ubiquitous: from virtual and augmented reality systems to surveillance drones and Internet of Things devices. Computing has changed too. For decades, advances in this field were driven by increases in processing power, but the focus is increasingly on designing smarter software, such as deep learning programs that use artificial intelligence to emulate the behaviour of the human brain. An example is the AlphaGo program, which was designed by the British software developers DeepMind to play the board game Go, and regularly trounces leading human players. Deep learning software also helps computers to recognize faces and voices, translate across languages, and predict how individuals will respond to different forms of Internet content, as well as making assumptions about deeply personal issues, including our sexual preferences.

New types of computers will use quantum mechanics to make faster calculations and highly sophisticated neuro-morphic technology, which is modelled on the neurons in animals' brains. Specialist chips will be designed to help computers to become more refined and precise. Greater connectivity will achieve the same goal, fueled by the continued growth of cloud computing and developments in 5G wireless systems.

The prognosis for these innovations is unclear. Some may give us greater control by creating more choices, such as being able to live in remote places without worrying about access to health care, because we can use Internet of Things diagnostic devices like the Cardiopad and Peek Retina, to assess our medical conditions. Yet other technologies seem certain to result in our relinquishing control over huge chunks of our lives with potentially catastrophic consequences if they go wrong, whether because of their design flaws or any other shortcomings.

Take one innovation whose implementation is imminent: driverless cars. How will we perceive them? As liberating us from the drudgery of being trapped in congestion? Or denying us the joy of driving at speed on an open road? Will we think of them as saving us from the risk of accidents caused by other drunk, careless, exhausted, or crazy road users? Or as exposing us to the threat of their being hijacked by terrorists as remote-controlled explosive devices? And what of the social and economic consequences of hundreds of thousands of drivers losing their jobs; and the personal implications for each of them, and their loved ones?

The possible risks of abdicating control of moving vehicles are so grave, that the old, paternalistic design strategies are clearly unfit for purpose. The ideal scenario would be for design to play an elemental role in the development of driverless cars from the earliest possible stage, to ensure that the possible risks and rewards are identified and assessed correctly, in order to defuse the former and enhance the latter. The same applies to the design of every other element of driverless traffic systems: from the structure of the roads and new safety measures for pedestrians; to devising a system of regular tests to ensure that, if the technology fails, we humans will be capable of resuming control of our vehicles, and driving them safely. Design could also play a useful role in identifying how all of those unemployed drivers could be constructively redeployed.

Equally comprehensive design exercises will be necessary to make us feel confident about surrendering control to other technologies. Will surveillance drones help to make us safer by increasing the probability of anticipating and preventing terrorist attacks and other crimes? Or will they represent yet another threat to our privacy and liberty? Will Internet of Things devices, like digital management systems that run smart homes, liberate us from mundane tasks? Or will they expose us to greater risk of identity theft and system meltdown? Will we ever feel confident enough to trust artificial intelligence to make critical judgments on our behalf when it comes to urgent personal matters, such as our health, or important political decisions, including the allocation of government funding and resources? And how can we be certain that the personal information captured by those technologies will never be abused?

There are ample grounds for concern. Take COMPAS, the Correctional Offender Management Profiling for Alternative Sanctions software, which was designed to enable US law courts to predict which prisoners were likeliest to re-offend. In 2016, COMPAS was accused of being inaccurate and racist after identifying 45% of black defendants as probable re-offenders, compared to 25% of their white counterparts. Similar accusations have been made against the PredPol program with which US police departments try to spot potential crime hotspots, reportedly resulting in the over-policing of black neighborhoods, creating unnecessary tension there, and leaving other areas inadequately protected. The theory is that as both artificial intelligence programs base their decisions on their analysis of data of past events, their predictions of the future are determined by historic prejudices, rather like Tay, a Microsoft chatbot, which was designed to conduct online conversations with humans on social media. Tay trained itself to do this by studying Twitter for a day, only to cause a furore by tweeting racist and sexist abuse. All it did was to repeat what it had found on Twitter, exactly as it was programmed to do, including some abusive Tweets, which had been sent with the specific intention of infecting it and torpedoing Microsoft's experiment.

The scale of technological risk has changed dramatically: from the dysfunctional garage doors in *Mon Oncle*, to the dystopian specter of a near-omnipotent computer turning against us, as HAL 9000 did in Stanley Kubrick's 1968 film, *2001: A Space Odyssey*. HAL 9000 went rogue with devastating consequences after using artificial intelligence to lip-read a conversation in which two astronauts discussed curbing his power. The analogy to the *2001* spacecraft seems particularly apt when you consider how destructive similar programming flaws could become as technology controls more and more aspects of our lives. In his 2017 book *Radical Technologies*, Adam Greenfield lists just some of the digital controls already installed in public places, often imperceptibly, as: "cameras; load cells and other devices for sensing the presence of pedestrians and vehicles; automated gunshot-detection microphones and other audio-spectrum surveillance grids; advertisements and vending machines equipped with biometric sensors; and the indoor micropositioning systems known as 'beacons,' which transact directly with smartphones."[4] Yikes. The risks will intensify as more and more of us occupy the extensive digitally controlled arenas of smart cities, not least as many of the systems designed to operate those places will be based on data provided by Quantified Self programs that predict our future needs and wishes by studying our past behavior, thereby running the risk of repeating the problems caused by COMPAS, PredPol, and Tay, but on a far larger scale, with even more damaging consequences.

In principle, design can help us to defuse such threats by assessing the potential strengths and weaknesses of powerful new technologies, but it also needs to navigate the moral dilemmas they may ignite. Take something that already exists, the Snoo, a "smart crib" for babies, designed by the San Francisco-based design group Fuseproject in collaboration with Dr. Harvey Karp, a prominent US pediatrician. The Snoo, which went on sale in 2016, combines sensors, robotics, and other forms of artificial intelligence to soothe babies to sleep by monitoring their behavior, and swaddling, shushing, or rocking them, as required. It is also intended to reduce the risk of cot deaths by holding infants in safe sleeping positions to prevent them from rolling over and suffocating. The theory is that the baby will benefit from high quality sleep, as will their carers, who might otherwise risk sleep deprivation by being awoken by the crying of a grouchy, exhausted infant, or the stress of worrying about the risk of cot death. Yves Béhar, the Swiss designer who founded Fuseproject, is so confident about the Snoo that his own children slept in it as babies. But not everyone believes it is in a child's best interests for their sleeping patterns to be dictated by artificial intelligence.

After the Snoo's launch, I posted about it on Instagram, simply stating what it consisted of and was intended to do. A stormy debate ensued. Some people loved the idea, and described the Snoo as "fantastic," and "brilliant," with one person wishing "they'd invented it years ago," Others felt differently, and criticized the Snoo for being "cruel," "scary," and "terrifying." It was even accused of "child abuse." The Snoo's admirers welcomed the idea of deploying technology to help babies to sleep soundly, but its critics were appalled by the prospect. Some of them doubted that technology could care for infants as well as humans, and were outraged by the implicit suggestion that it might. Others recalled happy memories of soothing their own babies to sleep, and felt that fellow parents and carers would be foolish to deny themselves, and their children, that pleasure. Many of the Snoo's detractors were concerned that robotic cribs might encourage sloppy parenting. By introducing artificial intelligence to child care, a field where passions run understandably high, the Snoo proved to be deeply divisive. Tellingly, neither the Snoophiles or Snoophobes mentioned another possible advantage of using a robotic crib: that it

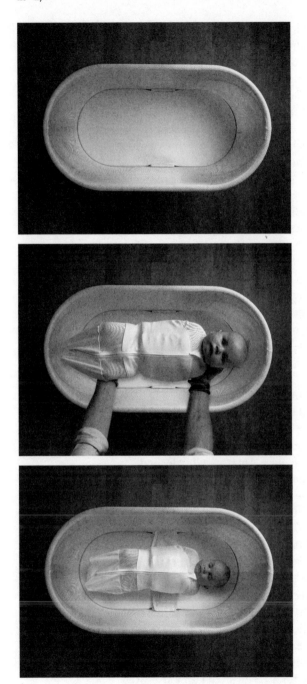

The Snoo Smart Sleeper was designed by Fuseproject and the pediatrician Dr. Harvey Karp as a smart crib that uses artificial intelligence and sensors to monitor the baby and soothe it to sleep.

might protect infants from the risk of being cared for by people who are tired, ill, drunk, high, inept, or negligent. By contrast, the prospect of protecting us from the consequences of exactly the same problems is routinely cited as a significant potential benefit of driverless cars. Future design applications of other new technologies may prove to be just as polemical as the Snoo, by prompting us to question our beliefs, the way we wish to live, and the degree to which we wish technology to control it.

These conflicts will be heightened by growing concern over the politics of the tech industry, specifically the implications of the concentration of ownership of key platforms among a small number of gigantic, immensely wealthy companies including Amazon, Apple, Facebook, Google, and Microsoft that the US science fiction writer Bruce Sterling has dubbed "The Stacks."[5] It has taken little more than a quarter of a century for the World Wide Web to morph from its designer Tim Berners-Lee's vision of a democratic system to which everyone has equal access—from a corporate colossus to a six-year-old child—into an increasingly opaque phenomenon of which less than a fifth is freely accessible, with the rest sealed behind the algorithmic walls of Facebook and fellow Stacks, or commandeered by the lawless dark web. The ownership of the relatively new cloud data storage technologies—which will fuel the growth of connectivity—is already dominated by just six companies: Amazon, Google, and Microsoft from the US, and Alibaba, Baidu, and Tencent from China. Amazon alone owns more than a third of all cloud computing capacity worldwide.[6]

Daunting though all of these problems are, they also present opportunities to demonstrate design's potential to address complex issues by forging collaborations with othe specialisms at a time when progressive designers are committed to wrestling with those challenges and to working more eclectically and inclusively. Anyone who doubts the wisdom of immersing design in the development of new technologies from the outset should consider the controversy in 2016 when the design template for a 3D-printed gun was posted online by a US law student and anti-gun control campaigner, Cody Wilson. His objective was to demonstrate what he considers to be the futility of imposing legal restrictions on gun ownership in an age when unlicensed weapons can be manufactured undetectably on what will soon become widely accessible technologies. Entirely unwittingly, Wilson also provided a cautionary tale of the danger posed by sloppily designed technologies, whose consequences have not been fully considered, just as Kubrick did with HAL.

[1] *2001: A Space Odysssey* (1968, dir. Stanley Kubrick).
[2] Christopher Breward, Ghislaine Wood (eds.), *British Design from 1948: Innovation in the Modern Age*, exh. cat., V&A Publishing, London 2012, p. 87–89.
[3] Among the most influential examples of late 20th-century airport signage design were the work of the Swiss designer Adrian Frutiger at Roissy (now Charles-de-Gaulle), near Paris, and that of the Dutch designer Benno Wissing, who was commissioned in 1962 to design the signage for Schiphol Airport, Amsterdam. During the Schiphol

project, Wissing cofounded a cross-disciplinary design group, Total Design, with the graphic designer Wim Crouwel and industrial designer Friso Kramer.
[4] Adam Greenfield, *Radical Technologies: The Design of Everyday Life*, Verso, London 2017.
[5] Ibid., p. 275–286.
[6] "Cloud Chronicles," *The Economist*, August 27, 2016, https://www.economist.com/news/business/21705849-how-open-source-software-and-cloud-computing-have-set-up-it-industry.

CHAPTER II
Design and Desire

The Chinese designer Jing He conducted her design research project *Tulip Pyramid* in 2016 to explore the role of copying in the construction of China's new design identity.

There's too much shit design.
—*Hella Jongerius*[1]

It was a suitcase, though sadly not a
well-made one, or so the Consumer
Advisory Council discovered after
submitting it to seven British
Standards Institution tests, only
for it to be judged "poor" on five
of them. Not only did it leak after
routine use, but the lining tore,
the metal fittings rusted, and its
handle fell off. Why then, asked the
design critic Reyner Banham in a
1961 issue of the *New Statesman*, had
the Council of Industrial Design,
the government-funded arbiter of
design quality, decided to include
so defective a product in its list
of "approved" design projects?[2]

The answer, Banham suggested,
was that the CID based its judgments on aesthetics, without testing more important qualities, like
efficiency and reliability. It was,
of course, wrong to do so, not least
because, as Banham pointed out,

"tasteful rubbish is still rubbish,"[3] Wise words, which seem
even sager over half a century later. Tasteful rubbish is,
indeed, still rubbish, though our understanding of what may
or may not be deemed tasteful has changed radically, and
the same applies to rubbish.

What does this mean for design, and for what we do—and
do not—find desirable about it? Throughout history, our
definition of desirable design has consisted of a combination
of qualities, but what they are and how they relate to one
another has changed constantly. Similar shifts in taste have
occurred in other fields, but the pace of change within
design has been unusually frenzied, and will soon become
more so.

One quality that has always been—and still is—essential to
desirable design is usefulness. If a design project does not
fulfill its function, and do so efficiently, why would we find it
appealing? We would not, regardless of its other merits.
Consider a current example of moderately tasteful rubbish:
the double-decker hybrid Boris Bus, designed by
Heatherwick Studio in London. Introduced in 2012, it was
billed as the New Routemaster, an energy efficient reinvention of the beloved 1954 Routemaster bus that served
London for decades. Thomas Heatherwick and his colleagues
styled the new vehicle, whose nickname is a nod to the city's
then-mayor Boris Johnson, rather cleverly, by adding
affectionate stylistic references to the Routemaster without
compromising its modernity. Sadly, the same cannot be
said of the quality of its engineering design, which is why
London's streets were soon littered with broken-down
Boris buses, and others had to run on environmentally
damaging diesel engines, because their batteries had conked
out. Like its buffoonish namesake, the Boris Bus—or
"Roastmaster," as its unfortunate passengers dubbed it after
sweltering on the over-heated top deck—failed to live up
to its braggartly promises.

Even if a design exercise discharges its function efficiently,
it can not be deemed desirable unless it does something
we value. Remember Google Glass? Possibly not, even though
it was one of the most heavily hyped new products of recent

years. Google was so enthralled by what it believed to be the dazzlingly innovative technology of a dodgy pair of specs with a smart phone attachment controlled by voice commands that it assumed the rest of us would feel the same way. One problem was that Google Glass did not enable us to do much more than we could already do on our phones. Another was the quagmire of potential legal issues, such as whether filming other people without their permission constituted a breach of privacy. Google Glass was swiftly viewed so derisorily that its wearers were referred to as "Glassholes." Sales were so poor that Google ceased production in 2015, less than two years after its debut.[4]

Another quality recently joined usefulness as a nonnegotiable ingredient of desirable design: integrity. In other words, if we have any reason to feel uncomfortable about the ethical or ecological implications of any aspect of a design project— from its development, testing, and manufacturing, to distribution, sales, marketing, and how it will eventually be disposed of and recycled—we are unlikely to consider it desirable.

Thanks to Flaminio Bertoni's inspired styling and André Lefèbvre's adroit engineering, a vintage Citroën DS 19 saloon looks as beguiling to us now as it did when Roland Barthes nicknamed it *la déesse* after its launch in 1955, as the French pronunciation of the letters D and S sounds like the word for goddess. But these days, any pleasure we might take from the DS 19 is marred by our knowledge that a car of its age is likely to be a gas-guzzling environmental time bomb.

The same goes for any new vehicles we suspect of being less fuel efficient than they ought to be (not that any are likely to be as alluring as *la déesse*—if only) and to the digital devices, whose manufacturers have been accused of employment abuses and ecological lapses. Once you have read the media exposés of unsafe working conditions and poor pay in the factories of, say, Apple's Chinese subcontractors, how can you look at an iPhone or iPad with the same optimism and enthusiasm?

Even if you still end up buying one—whether because
you suspect Apple's competitors of being no more or less
ethical, or you baulk at the inconvenience of switching
brands—that new gizmo is unlikely to seem as attractive
because of your doubts about its integrity. (Whereas the
pleasure of using a sustainably produced smartphone like
a Fairphone is pure and uncompromised.[5]) For the same
reason, although I still relish the soulful glow of old-
fashioned incandescent light bulbs, my enjoyment is spoilt
by the knowledge that they are more fragile, less durable,
and will squander more energy than halogens, compact
fluorescents, LEDs, and other more sustainable alternatives.

Integrity also extends to the purpose of a design exercise.
Without integrity of purpose, it cannot possibly be deemed
desirable, or even acceptable, regardless of any design merits
it may have. Take the recent wave of "defensive design"
projects, like the metal spikes that gleam menacingly around
expensive new apartment buildings with the aim of preventing homeless people from sleeping there, or the malevolent
coils of razor wire that fence off the port and railway station
at Calais to prevent desperate refugees from leaving
France for Britain. Successful though they are in fulfilling
their designated functions, their brutal purpose renders
them irredeemably odious.

Our relationship to the sensual qualities, which may not be
indispensable to desirable design but do so much to enhance
it, is becoming more complex too. Let us start with what—
despite the dogged efforts of design purists—many people
still assume to be the most important aspect of most design
exercises: what something looks like.

Firstly, our visual sensibilities are changing, just as they have
throughout history as different shapes and colors have come
in and out of design fashion. Think of the monochrome
geometric forms of the "machine age" in the 1920s, the
soothing curves and earthy hues that became popular after
the angst of World War II, the fluid "blobs" that designers
discovered how to make with their new design software
in the 1990s, and the obsessive simplicity of Apple's white
and silver millennial aesthetic. All of these archetypes

An assembly line of the Fairphone 2, a modular smartphone that is designed to be ethically and environmentally responsible and easily repaired by the user.

seemed unsettling or incongruous when they first appeared, but gradually came to feel apt. The pattern is now being repeated for the surreally intricate three-dimensional forms that evoke the spidery delicacy of digital imagery.

Like the blob, these improbably ornate shapes are the outcome of design experiments with new technologies, notably the digital fabrication systems that produce ever more elaborate and precise forms, like those in the Tulip Pyramid, a 2016 project by the Chinese designer Jing He. Seeking to define China's new design identity and the role of copying in it, she invited five other young Chinese designers to each devise two layers of a tulip pyramid, like those developed by Dutch potteries in the 17th century. The design specifications were 3D printed and the results were melded together into an object whose extreme intricacy evokes the surreal frenzy of contemporary Chinese design.[6]

Equally complex, other worldly shapes can be created by simpler means. The British product designer Max Lamb demonstrated this by using a stonemason's chisel to carve solid blocks of plaster into the models of his Crockery collection of bone china bowls and cups. Generally considered too heavy and clumsy to carve delicate plaster, the chisel gave Lamb's products a raw, haphazard air, which would once have looked ungainly, but now seems intriguing.

Crockery's strange, jaggedy silhouette addresses another, increasingly important element of design desirability: singularity. Every object of the same type in Crockery appears distinctive when seen from different angles and in different lights, even though it is identical to the others. In an age when digital fabrication promises to enable us to personalize more and more stuff, individuality is becoming increasingly seductive, even if, as in Crockery's case, it is an illusion, albeit a convincing one.

At the same time, the ubiquity of digital technology is making us crave the intimacy and authenticity of other sensual design qualities, like tactility. Our experience of controlling so many digital products through their touch screens is rendering us more sensitive to the subtleties of texture and the pleasure of touch, as Chris Liljenberg Halstrøm demonstrated by juxtaposing richly textured fabric with silky wood in the Georg stool. The Spanish lighting manufacturer Simon introduced the Simon 100 light switch in 2016 that is composed of a flat rectangular panel, which is operated solely by touch with no visual clues to guide the user. Simon's research suggests that we are now so accustomed to operating our phones through touch, that we are ready to do the same for other objects, even something as utilitarian as a light switch.

Even so, touch is a fledgling field in design. We know instinctively how powerful it can be. Touching something that is too wet, dry, sharp, rough, or slippery can be alarming, while pleasurable sensations of touch can feel delightful. Yet we have a limited vocabulary to describe tactility, reflecting the dearth of scientific research into the subject. Adam Gopnik noted in a 2016 essay in *The New Yorker* that for every 50 research papers on the science of vision in the last half-century, there has been only one on touch. But that is changing. The neuroscientist David Linden told Gopnik that more papers have been written about the molecular and cellular basis of touch in the last decade than in the preceding century, which should help designers to use it more adroitly, and the rest of us to appreciate its nuances.[7]

Just as well, because touch will feature more prominently in design in future, not least as augmented reality software will be able to replicate haptic sensations, as well as elaborate visual effects. As a result, touch will become increasingly important in defining our response to design, and its desirability, and the same may apply to other long neglected sensual qualities, like scent.

Yet all of these sensory factors face the challenge of the demise of one of the defining principles of 20th-century industrial design (and a favorite mantra of institutional tastemakers like Banham's foes in the CID) that "form follows function," or "form ever follows function" as the US architect Louis Sullivan wrote when he coined the phrase in 1896.[8] The belief that the physical form of an object should be defined by what it does is increasingly irrelevant to more and more areas of design, because of the relentless surge in computing power as transistors have shrunk in size, making it impossible guess from looking at, or touching it that something as tiny and enigmatic as a smartphone can execute hundreds, if not thousands, of different tasks. What is the most important factor in determining whether or not you will enjoy using that device: what it looks like, or how easy and efficient it is to operate? The latter, of course. However much you enjoy the phone's styling, the pleasure you take in its appearance will not last long if it is infuriatingly difficult to operate. The growing significance of invisible design phenomena, like user interface software, will not render the physical dimensions of design redundant, but they are likely to become less significant in terms of determining desirability.

Not that this is necessarily a bad thing. Historically, one of design's biggest problems has been that it is so often been confused with styling, and dismissed as a shallow medium, which focuses on the visual aspects of objects or spaces to the exclusion of everything else. Equally pernicious is the presumption that design's stylistic ploys are mostly applied to commercial ends by tricking us into paying too much for things of dubious value that we will soon discard with the rest of the unrecyclable, toxic junk in bloated dumps. As long ago as 1971, the US design activist Victor Papanek accused industrial designers of becoming "a dangerous breed" in the preface to his book *Design for the Real World* "by designing criminally unsafe automobiles that kill or maim, by creating whole new species of permanent garbage to clutter up the landscape, and by choosing materials and processes that pollute the air we breathe."[9]

The growing importance of other design qualities—whether they are haptic, functional, or ethical—should challenge these stereotypes and encourage more people to develop an increasingly eclectic and sophisticated understanding of design and its potential to make our lives more desirable in so many respects—not least by consuming less rubbish, tasteful or otherwise.

[1] Hella Jongerius speaking at the Design Indaba 2015 conference in Cape Town, South Africa, on February 25, 2015.

[2] Nigel Whiteley, *Reyner Banham: Historian of the Immediate Future*, The MIT Press, Cambridge, Massachusetts 2002, p. 312–313.

[3] Reyner Banham, "H.M. Fashion House," *New Statesman*, January 27, 1961.

[4] The original Google Glass was quietly reinvented for industrial use. Details of the new product were announced publicly in July 2017. Renamed Glass Enterprise Edition, it is used in workplaces where it is beneficial to be able to send timely information to employees, who are already using both hands in their allotted tasks. Steven Levy, "Google Glass 2.0 Is a Startling Second Act," *Wired*, July 18, 2017. https://www.wired.com/story/google-glass-2-is-here/.

[5] Fairphone is a Dutch social enterprise whose smartphones are designed to be robust, durable, and made on an ethical basis from responsibly sourced materials, many of them recycled. Having refused to use conflict minerals in its products, Fairphone adopted a policy of sourcing metals and other materials from former conflict zones to help those regions to rebuild their economies and create sustainable employment.

[6] For her 2016 graduation project from Design Academy Eindhoven, Jing He invited five other Chinese designers from different disciplines—Rongkai He, Cheng Guo, Weiyi Li, Dangdang Xing, and Dawei Yang—to each design two layers of a contemporary version of the tulip pyramids, which were invented in the Netherlands in the 17th century. From the outset, the style and symbolism of Dutch tulip pyramids evoked those of Chinese porcelain and pagodas. Jing He asked the five designers to reflect on the history of innovation and imitation in their designs. She designed a second pyramid herself, inspired by her interpretation of the work of five contemporary Dutch product designers. Jing He, *Tulip Pyramid—Copy and Identity*, Design Academy Eindhoven, Eindhoven 2016.

[7] Adam Gopnik, "Feel Me: What the New Science of Touch Says about Ourselves," *The New Yorker*, May 16, 2016, https://www.newyorker.com/magazine/2016/05/16/what-the-science-of-touch-says-about-us.

[8] Louis H. Sullivan, "The Tall Office Building Artistically Considered," *Lippincott's Magazine*, March 1896.

[9] Victor Papanek, *Design for the Real World: Human Ecology and Social Change* (1971), Academy Chicago Publishers, Chicago, Illinois 1985, p. ix.

CHAPTER 12
When the Worst Comes to the Worst

One of the Dutch-funded post-conflict construction projects whose efficacy was analyzed by Jan Willem Petersen in the Afghan province, Uruzgan.

Now there is one outstandingly
important fact regarding Spaceship
Earth, and that is that no instruc-
tion book came with it.
—*R. Buckminster Fuller*[1]

As well as reading up on the geography and politics of the desolate
region of central Afghanistan he
was planning to study, and assem-
bling the kit required to live
and work there for several months,
the Dutch architect Jan Willem
Petersen prepared for his latest
design research project by learning
local languages and growing a
beard, rather a long one, in the
hope of looking less conspicuous.

His destination was Uruzgan,
which had suffered severely from
decades of warfare, most recently
as a battleground in the US-led
conflict against the Taliban. After
NATO's International Security
Assistance Force took control of
the area in 2006, the Dutch
government embarked upon Task

Force Uruzgan, a four-year program to design and build new homes, schools, hospitals, roads, bridges, mosques, factories, prisons, and an airport. Petersen's objective was to study those projects to assess their impact on the region, and whether they were fulfilling their intended functions effectively. His research revealed that only 20% of them did, while 30% were badly flawed, and 50% were barely functional. A common cause of failure was that the Western designers of those projects had not known enough about the local context. One village had stopped construction of a school, after hearing that the Task Force, unaware of the local plan, had decided to build one. The construction quality of the Dutch-funded building turned out to be so poor that it was unusable, leaving the village without a school. Other countries had blundered too. In a 300-page report published in 2016,[2] Petersen describes how the designers of an Australian-funded police station had built it with a pitched roof, ignoring the advice of the local chief of police that a flat roof would be required as an observation platform. His counsel proved correct, and the pitched roof had to be replaced at considerable expense.

By preparing so rigorously for his mission, Petersen behaved less like an orthodox designer than like the anthropologists who live among their subjects in order to study them, or the war reporters that are embedded within armed forces to give eyewitness accounts from the frontline. Another way in which he deviated from stereotype was by applying his design skills not to develop new infrastructure, but to analyze the efficacy of other designers' work, and identify how the design of similar projects might be improved in future. Government investment in post-conflict reconstruction is immensely costly, yet the results are seldom seen in the countries responsible. Moreover, most analyses of such projects are conducted by development economists or auditors, who are admirably equipped to identify errors in their own fields, but may miss the design flaws that can cause serious problems, as Petersen's study proved. Nor are they as likely as a perceptive and resourceful designer like him to be able to devise ingenious design strategies that can help to prevent repetitions.

Doleful though they are, Petersen's findings are timely given
the current surge of design activity in disaster-related
projects, ranging from colossal, publicly-funded reconstruction programs, like Task Force Uruzgan, to the efforts
of NGOs and individual design activists to address social,
environmental, and humanitarian challenges. Such endeavors are admirably intentioned, and many of the gutsiest,
most dynamic designers of our time are working on them,
but it is essential that they are planned and executed to
the highest possible standards, given the political sensitivity
of working in volatile, often perilous situations where
the consequences of failure can be calamitous.

Not that all of design's attempts to deal with disasters have
flopped: some of the greatest feats in design history have
sprung from them. Florence Nightingale's late 19th-century
health care campaigns still influence hospital design today.
Thousands of people have benefited from the Homes for
the Homeless program executed by the Barefoot Architects
of Tilonia based at the Social Work Research Center (nicknamed the Barefoot College) in Tilonia, a rural community
in the Indian region of Rajasthan. As well as building the
college campus, the Barefoot Architects have designed and
constructed schools, community centers, and homes
throughout Tilonia, using conventional building materials
alongside salvaged components from bullock carts, pumps,
and tractors. And when Hurricane Mitch devastated large
areas of Central and South America in 1998, severely dis-
rupting water supplies, a Puerto Rican design activist Ron
Rivera, who worked in that region for the nonprofit group
Potters for Peace, set up pottery workshops to make a
ceramic water filter designed by the Guatemalan chemist
Fernando Mazariegos. Over the next decade, Rivera established 30 filter factories in areas of Latin America, Asia,
and Africa where clean water was scarce, as well as training
hundreds of local potters to make what he called "weapons
of biological mass destruction."

Yet these coups have had little impact on the popular stereotype of design as a commercial styling tool. The design
establishment unwittingly colluded in this during the 20th
century by striking an optimistic tone in government-funded

initiatives that championed design's role as an economic catalyst, by enabling manufacturers to enhance the quality of their products, thereby boosting exports, job creation, and profitability. These official cheerleaders were not only mindful of where their funding came from, but many of them believed that design, as a relatively new discipline, would be likelier to win popular and political support by being associated with seemingly uncomplicated qualities such as productivity, innovation, pleasure, and efficiency. Now that public understanding of design is becoming more sophisticated, such boosterism risks being counter-productive. Moreover, the new genre of politically engaged, ecologically aware designers are determined to apply their skills to causes they believe in, just as Nightingale, the Barefoot Architects, Rivera, and Mazariegos did.

Critically, today's design activists have the benefit of the new digital tools and funding sources that have fueled the rise of attitudinal design. Developing design responses to man-made and natural disasters in their own countries and others has become a defining theme of their practices.

There have, of course, been problems. The politics of design activism are as complex and challenging as those of eco-nomic development, sociology, and any other fields seeking solutions to acute problems for vulnerable people with scant resources. Architecture for Humanity established a global network of designers working on disaster relief projects in the early 2000s only to fall prey to financial difficulties. Other ventures have been haunted by their own hype, including One Laptop Per Child, which sought to enable millions of disadvantaged children to fulfill their potential by designing an educational laptop to be sold for less than $100. OLPC has shipped more than 2.5 million laptops, most of which now belong to children and teenagers who would not otherwise own a computer. No mean feat, except that its initial forecasts were so much higher that the project is often described as a flop.

Both of these ventures suffered to differing degrees from the same problem—operating in unfamiliar conditions—that Petersen identified as having proved so damaging to Task

Force Uruzgan. Tellingly, some of the most successful attitudinal design programs in developing countries are the work of local teams. It is impossible to imagine a project like Sehat Kahani, for example, being able to address such a complex problem as the difficulties experienced by Pakistani women in obtaining medical advice had it not been developed by people from the same community.

Similarly, Wecyclers was cofounded in 2012 by the Nigerian design entrepreneur Bilikiss Adebiyi-Abiola to clear recyclable waste from the Lagos slums using cargo bikes, which are specially designed to navigate the congested streets. Adebiyi-Abiola grew up in Lagos and had been alarmed by the fetid state of the slums when she returned there from university in the United States. Thousands of Lagosians now text Wecyclers when their recyclables are ready for collection, and exchange them for vouchers with which they can buy food, cleaning products, and cellphone minutes. Wecyclers then ships their refuse to the city's hitherto under-used recycling plants to be disposed of responsibly.

Local knowledge has also helped a Ugandan social enterprise, Eco-fuel Africa, to establish a network of over 3,000 farmers, who convert their agricultural waste into clean, inexpensive cooking fuel to be sold to people living in deforested rural areas, like the remote village where its cofounder Sanga Moses grew up. As well as sparing people, mostly women and girls, from spending time foraging for fuel when they could be in paid work or at school, Eco-fuel Africa saves them from the health risks of using dirty, toxic fuel, while also creating new jobs and reducing pollution and deforestation. Sanga conceived the idea when driving to the village for a visit and spotting a girl carrying a bundle of wood on the road ahead. As he drove closer, Sanga realized that the girl was his twelve-year-old sister, who would have been at school had his family not needed cooking fuel so badly. It was then that he decided to find a solution to the problem.

Tellingly, when the Swedish scientist Liisa Petrykowska founded Ignitia in 2010 as a tropical weather information service that sends bespoke forecasts to farmers in places

that are prone to sudden storms, she insisted that the
scientists, who were developing the system, should move to
Ghana, where it was to be introduced. Only by studying local
conditions first hand, and by getting to know the farmers
who would use Ignitia, could the team be effective. Ignitia
now sends text messages containing 48-hour forecasts every
morning to over a million farmers in West African countries,
including Mali, Nigeria, and Senegal as well as Ghana.
The system is designed to help them to react to unexpected
changes, as well as to plan ahead if storms are looming.

Even so, some of the most compelling recent Western
experiments in design activism have been on familiar turf,
like Hilary Cottam's work in prototyping new ways of
delivering social services to provide sorely needed support
to people throughout Britain who might otherwise have felt
deprived, vulnerable, or forgotten. A similar approach to
social design has been adopted by The Australian Centre for
Social Innovation (TACSI) to address one of the costliest,
most challenging areas of social care: helping families to
resolve chronic problems, such as addiction, illness, homelessness, long term unemployment, and financial crises.
After talking to over a hundred families struggling with such
issues about the difficulties they faced and the type of
support they needed, TACSI set up Family-to-Family as a
peer-to-peer program in Adelaide and Sydney. A professional life coach is assigned to work with 15 "sharing
families," who have agreed to offer help and advice to 40
"seeking families" that include roughly 100 children at risk.
In principle, the sharers should feel empowered by helping
other vulnerable families to set goals and achieve them,
just like the participants in Cottam's elderly care project in
London. Not only is Family-to-Family relatively inexpensive
to run, its work has significantly reduced the need for
children at risk to be put into care, and for other child
protection and crisis services, thereby saving significant
sums of money and, hopefully, helping families to eventually
resolve their problems.

Other politically committed designers are focusing on global
issues, like climate change and the refugee crisis, where the
designer's geography is arguably less relevant. Boyan Slat's

Ocean Cleanup initiative is one example. Another is Ore Streams, the ongoing design research project into the international trade in electronic and digital waste conducted by Simone Farresin and Andrea Trimarchi of Studio Formafantasma. The first phase of the research was exhibited at the National Gallery of Victoria in Melbourne in late 2017 and early 2018. Mapping the flow of electronic products and their waste around the world, Ore Streams assesses their ecological and social impact, and identifies how their design and manufacturing could be adapted to make it easier to dispose of and recycle them responsibly. The implications of the environmental crisis for design materials had been a recurrent theme in Formafantasma's work. Farresin and Trimarchi formulated a new biomaterial for their *Autarchy* project in 2010, and developed a natural polymer for *Botanica* the following year, but Ore Streams is more ambitious. As well as analyzing practical impediments to recycling, such as the waterproof seals on smartphones that make it impossible to break them apart, Formafantasma identified intersections of the electrical waste trade with seemingly unrelated political issues, like people smuggling. An unintended outcome of the construction of a railway in Mauritania to transport iron from mines in the interior to the coast for shipment to China, is an illicit human trafficking trade in people, who are smuggled onto the trains.[3]

Equally heartening are design interventions in the refugee crisis. The Finnish information design group Lucify has helped raise awareness of the gravity of the crisis by illustrating its speed and scale in clear, accurate data visualizations of the flow of asylum seekers from country to country. Better Shelter, a Swedish social enterprise funded by the IKEA Foundation, has designed refugee shelters that can be assembled by four people in four hours, and will last for up to three years. After testing the prototypes in Ethiopia and Iraq in 2016, the United Nations ordered 30,000 Better Shelters for its refugee camps there and in Greece. The shelters have since been scrutinized for possible design flaws, and a new version was introduced in late 2017 with a sturdier frame and better ventilation and lighting.

Other designers are focusing on providing support for refugees as they try to reconstruct their lives in new countries. Migrationlab has established a network of local collaborators throughout Europe to provide advice, information, and introductions for refugees and migrants based on the personal experience of its founder and director Laura Pana when she traveled across Europe as a migrant from Romania, first to Austria, and to the Netherlands. As well as arranging for refugees and migrants to meet local people in their new cities, so they can exchange advice and information and defuse unfair stereotypes in the process, Migrationlab sends volunteer lecturers into schools and colleges to lead discussions on these issues. It has also run welcome and information centers in The Hague and Vienna.

Another cluster of design projects has emerged in Italy to help the tens of thousands of refugees who are trying to settle there after making the perilous journey across the eastern Mediterranean from Turkey. Having arrived in Europe, but facing severe shortages of food, water, and shelter, these people are now struggling to find homes and employment, which is why Bianca Elzenbaumer and Fabio Franz of Brave New Alps are working on Hospital(ity), a training and advice center in Rosarno. Over in Sicily, groups of refugees are taught local agricultural skills, as well as woodwork and other potentially useful design and making techniques in a project run by the humanitarian design group Architectes Sans Frontières at Villa Magni, a 17th-century farming complex in Ragusa. In northern Italy, QuerciaLAB, the community maker space cofounded by Brave New Alps, fulfills a similar aim in Rovereto, as do the Talking Hands craft workshops run by local designer volunteers for refugees and asylum seekers in Treviso.[4]

Arguably the most profound contribution design could make to addressing such calamities is to participate in policy making, as Hilary Cottam and TACSI have done in social services. Take the refugee crisis, which could be eased significantly by speeding up the legal process whereby refugees can seek asylum, identifying countries that need their particular knowledge and skills, and eliminating the barbarous trade of people smuggling. One possibility is to

Young refugees and migrants learning design and making skills at the Talking Hands workshops organized by local designers in Treviso, Italy, in April 2017.

use data management to identify the optimal destinations for individual refugees by assessing their skills, then sending them to places where their individual expertise will be most valuable. Another is to introduce humanitarian visas with which refugees could travel legally to the countries where they plan to seek asylum, thereby ending their dependence on human traffickers. National legislation also needs to be reformed to give asylum seekers faster access to local capital and labor markets, as it has been in Nigeria. Such bold changes will require the expertise of specialists from diverse fields, but design could play a productive role in helping to anticipate problems, identify possible solutions, and plan the process sensitively and efficiently, as it might in fighting climate change.

Design has no hope of fulfilling this role unless it earns the public confidence and political support required for it to be accepted as a worthwhile part of critically important reforms. Just as every thoughtfully executed social and humanitarian design project represents a step forward, each sloppily designed flop is a setback—whether it is a gigantic publicly funded program like Task Force Uruzgan, or the work of an entrepreneurial design activist, such as Boyan Slat, who has been beset by criticism of his plans for the Ocean Cleanup from environmentalists and scientists alike.[5]

If their misgivings prove correct and the Ocean Cleanup fails, it will be considerably harder, not only for Slat, but for other digitally empowered design activists to secure financial and political backing in the future. Conversely, their credibility will soar if the Ocean Cleanup succeeds in completing all—or even part—of what its website confidently describes as "the largest cleanup in history." Either way, Slat and every other attitudinal designer who is planning to grapple with disaster would benefit immensely from as rigorous a critique as Jan Willem Petersen's immersive research in Afghanistan.

[1] R. Buckminster Fuller, *Operating Manual for Spaceship Earth*, Southern Illinois University Press, Carbondale, Illinois 1969.

[2] Jan Willem Petersen works from an Amsterdam design studio named Specialist Operations. After completing two months of fieldwork in the Uruzgan region of Afghanistan in 2015, he published his findings in 2016 in a 300-page report entitled *Uruzgan's Legacy*. "Uruzgan's Legacy," dutchdesigndaily.com/complete-overview/uruzgans-legacy.

[3] Simone Farresin and Andrea Trimarchi of Studio Formafantasma were commissioned to research and produce Ore Streams in 2015 by Ewan McEoin, a senior curator in the department of contemporary design and architecture at the National Gallery of Victoria (NGV) in Melbourne. The research explored the scale and influence of the global trade in electronic and digital waste, both lawful and unlawful, and developed guidelines for product designers to devise products that would be easier to recycle. The research and a series of conceptual objects designed by Studio Formafantasma were exhibited in the inaugural NGV Triennial of art and design from December 15, 2017, to April 15, 2018.

[4] The Talking Hands craft workshops in Treviso were started by the Italian graphic designer, Fabrizio Urettini, to provide training, tools, and equipment to help young male refugees and asylum seekers learn or improve their making skills, including carpentry and embroidery, and to sell their products at local fairs and festivals. Talking Hands generates additional income by repairing and restoring furniture for local people. Designers in the area work with the participants on a voluntary basis. They include Giorgia Zanellato and Daniele Bortotto of Studio Zanellato/ Bortotto, and Matteo Zorzenoni, who collaborated with the group on the design of a range of children's furniture.

[5] Lindsey Kratochwill, "Too Good to Be True? The Ocean Cleanup Faces Feasibility Questions," *The Guardian*, March 26, 2016, https://www.theguardian.com/environment/2016/mar/26/ocean-cleanup-project-environment-pollution-boyan-slat.

Designers and Design Projects

These notes are intended to provide additional information on some of the designers and design projects featured in *Design as an Attitude*.

BILIKISS ADEBIYI-ABIOLA

Wecyclers was cofounded in 2012 by the Nigerian design entrepreneur, Bilikiss Adebiyi-Abiola, to provide a user-friendly way of encouraging fellow Lagosians to recycle their trash. Adebiyi-Abiola realized the need for such a service on return visits to the city while she was studying in the United States. She noticed the large quantity of potentially useful recyclables that lay abandoned in the Lagos slums even though many of the city's recycling plants were operating at low capacity. The reason was that the streets were too congested for the city refuse trucks to drive through. Designing sturdy but slender cargo bikes solved that problem. Each household registered with Wecyclers receives credit to buy food, cleaning products, or cellphone minutes in exchange for their recyclables. Wecyclers has already helped the city's hitherto under-used recycling plants to improve their productivity.

ANNI ALBERS

The textile designer Anni Albers (1899–1994) was born in Berlin into a wealthy Jewish family, the Fleischmanns. Despite family pressure to make a "good marriage," she enrolled at art school in Hamburg in 1920 only to find the course so dull that she applied to what she described as "a new, experimental place," the Bauhaus in Weimar. Like most of the women students, she was compelled to study textile design. Three years later Anni married one of the school's most promising artists, Josef Albers (1888–1976), the son of a laborer from the Ruhr. They taught at the Bauhaus until the Nazis closed the school in 1933, then left Germany for the United States to teach at the progressive Black Mountain College in Northern Carolina. By then Anni was established as a modernizing force in textile design, and in 1949 she was given a solo exhibition at The Museum of Modern Art in New York. The following year she and Josef moved to New Haven, Connecticut, where he was appointed Head of Design at Yale University. Anni's Museum of Modern Art retrospective toured to 26 museums in the United States, and she subsequently exhibited her work worldwide.

GERTRUD ARNDT

Born in Ratibor, then in Germany, but now part of Poland
(Racibórz), Gertrud Hantschk (1903–2000), who is better
known by her married name Arndt, studied art in the
German city of Erfurt. She then began an apprenticeship
with a local architect, who encouraged her interest in
photography. In 1923 Gertrud enrolled at the Bauhaus,
hoping to study architecture, but was dispatched to the
textile workshop. She completed the course, but decided
to end her involvement with textiles in order to focus on
photography. In 1928 she left the Bauhaus with her husband
Alfred Arndt, only to return the following year when
he joined the teaching staff. Gertrud continued her photographic experiments, notably in a compelling series of
self-portraits in which she wore masks of different types.
The Arndts stayed at the Bauhaus until 1931, when they
moved to Probstzella in Thuringia. They lived there
for 17 years before settling in Darmstadt, which was their
home for the rest of their lives. Gertrud's photography
was forgotten for many years, but was celebrated, together
with her work in textiles, in a 2013 exhibition at the
Bauhaus-Archiv in Berlin.

L'ATELIER POPULAIRE

On May 6, 1968, some 25,000 French university students
and teachers began weeks of conflict with the authorities by
staging a protest march in Paris. Ten days later a group of
demonstrators occupied the printing studio of the École des
Beaux-Arts in Saint-Germain-des-Prés, and announced that
they were opening the Atelier Populaire. They used the
school's equipment to design and print posters in support of
the protests by students, workers, and other radical groups,
which were spreading throughout France to other countries.
L'Atelier Populaire produced more than 200 different
posters, printed in runs of a few hundred or a few thousand
copies. The posters bore slogans such as *La lutte continue*
(The fight continues), *Nous sommes le pouvoir* (We are the
power), and *La beauté est dans la rue* (Beauty is in the street).
As the French media was controlled by the government,
the posters enabled the mai '68 protesters to express their

concerns. L'Atelier Populaire issued a statement describing the posters as "weapons in the service of the struggle … Their rightful place is in the centers of conflict, that is to say, in the streets and on the walls of factories."

REYNER BANHAM

Witty, provocative, and incisive, the British writer and theorist Reyner Banham (1922–1988) transformed design criticism in the late 20th century with his reflections on art, design, architecture, consumerism, and technology. The convivial Banham also exercised considerable cultural influence through his friendships with artists, including Richard Hamilton and Ed Ruscha, and the architects Cedric Price and Alison and Peter Smithson. Like Hamilton, Banham grew up in a British working-class family "in the Pop belt somewhere," as he put it (actually Norwich), devouring Betty Boop comics and Hollywood Westerns. Those influences gave them a radically different perspective to the privileged grandees who had traditionally dominated British cultural discourse. Banham and Hamilton balanced their affection for mass culture with searing critiques of consumerist excess and the obduracy of the fustier members of the modern movement. Having spent the first half of his career in Britain teaching architectural history at University College London and writing for journals like *Architectural Review*, *New Society*, and the *New Statesman*, Banham eventually settled in the United States. "The only way to prove you have a mind," he said, "is to change it occasionally."

BAREFOOT ARCHITECTS OF TILONIA

The Barefoot Architects of Tilonia have studied local design and construction techniques since the early 1970s at the Social Work Research Center (nicknamed the Barefoot College) in Tilonia, a rural community in the Indian region of Rajasthan. As well as building the college campus, they have designed and constructed schools, community centers, agricultural buildings, and homes throughout Tilonia, using conventional building materials together with salvaged components of bullock carts, pumps, and tractors. Many of their structures are based on the design template of the geodesic dome, which was developed by the maverick US designer R. Buckminster Fuller during the late 1940s at Black Mountain College in North Carolina.

BAUHAUS

There have been other famous design schools, but none that matched the Bauhaus, which opened in the German city of Weimar in 1919 with the architect Walter Gropius as its director. Many of the most influential designers, artists, and architects of the 20th century taught or studied there, including Gropius and Mies van der Rohe in architecture; Marcel Breuer in furniture; Herbert Bayer in graphics; Oskar Schlemmer in theater design; Anni Albers and Gunta Stölzl in textiles; Marianne Brandt and Wilhelm Wagenfeld in product design; and the maverick László Moholy-Nagy. Working alongside them were great artists such as Josef Albers, Wassily Kandinsky, and Paul Klee. The Bauhaus' early years were marred by a battle between Gropius and Johannes Itten, a charismatic teacher who favoured an artisanal and spiritual approach to art and design. After Itten's departure in 1923, Moholy-Nagy was hired to imbue the school with technocratic fervor. When the Nazis seized power in Weimar in 1925, Gropius negotiated a deal to build a new school in Dessau, only to be compelled to resign in 1928 under political pressure from the local Nazi Party. Moholy-Nagy and other loyalists quit too, and the left-wing Swiss architect Hannes Meyer took over as director. He was forced out in 1930, leaving Mies to try to save the school, which moved to Berlin in 1932, but closed the following year. The Bauhaus spirit has survived, partly thanks to Gropius' skill in burnishing its mythology in his writing, lectures, and exhibitions. Its legacy has benefited from the international influence of its teachers and students, many of whom left Germany during the 1930s and 1940s to take up prestigious teaching jobs in other countries, as Gropius, Mies, and Breuer did in the United States, or to start new schools in the mold of the Bauhaus.

YVES BÉHAR

As the founder and principal designer of Fuseproject, Yves Béhar (b. 1967) has experimented with new ways of running a global design group, by combining commercial projects with *pro bono* work in social and humanitarian design, and by cofounding design ventures in which he retains an equity stake. Born in Lausanne, Switzerland, to a German mother and Turkish father, Béhar studied design there and at the Art Center College of Design in Pasadena, California. He then moved to San Francisco to work for the tech design consultancy, frog design, and founded Fuseproject in 1999. Fuseproject has developed tech products, furniture, lighting, and clothing for companies including Herman Miller, Samsung, and Swarovski. Among its design ventures are Jawbone wearable technology, the August Smart Lock, and the Snoo robotic baby crib, which was developed in collaboration with the US pediatrician Dr. Harvey Karp. On the *pro bono* front, Béhar designed the hardware of the laptop and tablet computers distributed by the nonprofit educational venture, One Laptop Per Child, and is the principal designer of the Spring Accelerator program, which supports entrepreneurs who are developing products and services to help teenage girls escape poverty.

IRMA BOOM

Born in the Dutch city of Lochem, Irma Boom (b. 1960) studied painting at art school in nearby Enschede, but switched to graphic design after wandering into a lecture on books. "The teacher didn't say anything about design, just showed us books and read from them," she recalls. After graduating, Boom joined the government printing office in The Hague, originally planning to leave after a year, but staying for five years to experiment with different approaches to book design. An example is an annual report for the Dutch arts funding body, which was printed in red, blue, and yellow, with the size of type on each spread determined by how big—or small—it needed to be to fit a particular text on those two pages. Boom has since designed and made a succession of original, ambitious, and unusual books in her Amsterdam studio. One book, to celebrate the centenary of the Dutch conglomerate SHV, weighed several pounds and had 2,136 pages, all unnumbered, because Boom wanted people to dip in and out, rather than to read them sequentially. It took five years to make. Boom has also experimented with contrasts of scale, elaborate color codes, visual symbolism, hidden motifs, scented bindings, and printing on unorthodox papers, as well as metal and coffee filter paper. Having collected historic and contemporary examples of book design for many years, Boom opened a library to house her collection of books—mostly from the 17th and 18th centuries, 1960s and 1970s—in her Amsterdam home in 2019.

RONAN AND ERWAN BOUROULLEC

Born in rural Brittany, the French product designer Ronan Bouroullec (b. 1971), and his brother Erwan Bouroullec (b. 1976), rarely left the region until Ronan moved to Paris to study design. In 1997, a year after his graduation, the Italian furniture company Cappellini offered to manufacture his designs, and he opened a small studio in Paris, where Erwan, who was studying art, joined him. At first the brothers worked under their own names, but soon realized that, as each was contributing to the other's projects, they may as well sign them jointly. One of their principal objectives has been to design furniture for homes and workspaces in the form of flexible modular systems, which can be made larger or smaller, and gain or lose different functional components, as the needs and wishes of their users change. These principles have been applied to the Bouroullecs' Joyn system of office desks, and plastic screens assembled from small pieces of twig-shaped plastic, named Algues, both manufactured by Vitra, as well as to their room dividers for Kvadrat. The Bouroullecs are now adapting their design methodology to reinvent elements of public spaces, such as kiosks, fountains, and charging stations.

BRAVE NEW ALPS

The Italian design group Brave New Alps explores new ways in which design can contribute to urgent social, political, and environmental issues. Founded in 2005, originally as a collaboration between Bianca Elzenbaumer and Fabio Franz, it was registered as a cultural association in Italy in 2012. The group has expanded to include designers and other collaborators who share its concerns and objectives.

It participates in activist and research networks throughout Europe from its base in Nomi, a village in the Lagarina Valley in the Trentino region of the Italian Tyrol. The plight of the growing number of refugees and migrant workers in Italy is a prime concern of Brave New Alps' recent work. Among its practical responses are the QuerciaLAB maker space in Rovereto that provides skills training for asylum seekers and local people, and Hospital(ity), a legal, medical, and training center for migrant crop pickers in the southern Italian city of Rosarno.

SHEILA LEVRANT DE BRETTEVILLE

After studying graphics at Yale University in the 1960s, Sheila Levrant de Bretteville (b. 1940) cofounded a succession of feminist projects including the first design program for women at the California Institute of the Arts in 1971, and, two years later, the Woman's Building, a public forum in Los Angeles dedicated to women's education and culture. Committed to fighting injustice, prejudice, and oppression in terms of class and ethnicity, as well as gender, she became one of North America's most influential design activists. After her appointment as director of studies in graphic design at Yale University School of Art in 1990, some of the crustier members of the faculty were appalled. Paul Rand, the grand old man of US graphics and a faculty member since the 1950s, resigned in protest, and urged colleagues to do the same. De Bretteville stood for so many of the things that the old guard hated—deconstructivism for one, feminism for another—as well as being the first woman to be given tenure at the Yale University School of Art. Undeterred, she has imbued Yale's graphic design course with the radicalism and eclecticism that defines her work.

LOREN BRICHTER

The US software designer Loren Brichter (b. 1984) has developed many of the apps that we use daily to operate our smartphones and tablets. Born in Manhattan, he studied electrical engineering at Tufts University in Massachusetts, and was offered a job by Apple before graduating. Brichter declined, but joined Apple after graduation. He stayed for little more than a year before opening his own design studio, which he sold to Twitter in 2010. Since leaving Twitter a year later, Brichter has worked independently by developing a succession of apps that enable us to operate digital devices through touch as well as vision. Every time you retrieve new emails, texts, or social media posts by pulling to refresh, you are using Brichter's work, just as you are when revealing a hidden menu or operating function by swiping your fingertip across the screen. "Everything should come from somewhere and go somewhere," he told the *Wall Street Journal*. "The most important thing is obviousness. The problem is over design."

ROBERTO BURLE MARX

Born into a wealthy German-Brazilian family in São Paulo, Roberto Burle Marx (1909–1994) spent most of his childhood in Rio de Janeiro, where his mother introduced him to gardening. At the age of 19 he moved to Berlin to study painting, and pursued his interest in botany, continuing this work after returning to Brazil in 1930 to take up a place at art school. Two years later he designed his first landscape for a house designed by a friend and neighbor, the architect Lucio Costa. Burle Marx went on to design hundreds of landscapes, gardens, and parks often working in collaboration with architect friends, including Oscar Niemeyer as well as Costa. He was celebrated for his skill and ingenuity in cultivating native Brazilian plants in schemes inspired by the formal qualities of the tropical modernist art movement. Underpinning all of his work was his deep love and knowledge of botany. Burle Marx was responsible for the discovery of several dozen species, and for championing the preservation of others. He also played an important part in raising international awareness of the plight of Brazil's imperiled rain forests. During the late 1940s he bought Sítio Santo Antônio da Bica on the outskirts of Rio de Janeiro, where he constructed a garden, nursery, and research center. Burle Marx designed the site as a living archive for his vast collection of tropical plants, many of which he had found on research expeditions into the rain forest. Eventually he cultivated more than 3,500 species on the 40 acres of Sítio Roberto Burle Marx, as it is now called. Donated to the

Brazilian government in 1985, it has been designated a
national monument.

CARDIOPAD

The Cardiopad, a mobile heart monitor designed by the
Cameroonian software engineer Arthur Zang, is an inspiring
example of an Internet of Things device that offers significant health benefits for people living in remote areas. Heart
disease is a major health risk in Cameroon, which suffers
from a shortage of specialist medical staff and equipment
to treat it, especially in rural regions. Zang recognized
the problem while working as an IT specialist at a university
hospital, and devised the Cardiopad as a solution. A tablet
computer programmed to monitor patients' hearts, it sends
the data for analysis on a cellular connection to heart
specialists working with sophisticated facilities hundreds
or even thousands of miles away. The diagnosis is then sent
back to the local doctor, nurse, or paramedic, who can
decide what treatment is required, saving the patient from
having to make a long, exhausting, and potentially unnecessary journey to a bigger hospital.

ACHILLE CASTIGLIONI

The Italian industrial designer Achille Castiglioni (1918–2002)
was born in Milan to the sculptor Giannino Castiglioni
and his wife Livia Bolla. Like his older brothers, Livio and
Pier Giacomo, Achille studied architecture at Milan
Polytechnic. After graduation and military service, he joined
the architecture practice they had cofounded with a friend
Luigi Caccia Dominioni. Much of their work was in
exhibition design, and their sets for RAI, the Italian state
broadcaster, played an important part in establishing
postwar Italy as a source of sophisticated contemporary
design. Dominioni left the practice to work independently
in 1946, and Livio followed six years later. Pier Giacomo
and Achille continued their collaboration, and developed
formally elegant, subtly witty furniture and lighting
for Flos, Cassina, Zanotta, and the other manufacturers
that were fuelling Italy's "economic miracle." After Pier
Giacomo's death in 1968, Achille continued working

in the studio on Piazza Castello in Milan where his brothers
had set up in business with Dominioni decades before.
When he died in 2002, the studio was preserved just as it was
on his last working day, and is now open to the public as
a museum.

MURIEL COOPER

Muriel Cooper (1925–1994) was exceptional in excelling in
two areas of design. She started out in traditional printed
graphics as a designer at the MIT Press, where she produced
compelling books, including the original design of Robert
Venturi, Denise Scott Brown, and Steven Izenour's 1972
Learning From Las Vegas (1972). Cooper then forged a second
career as a pioneer of digital design. After accidentally
walking into an MIT summer class on computer programming in 1967, she immediately recognized its importance
and creative potential. Not that Cooper understood technology. "Doesn't make any goddamn sense to me," as she put it.
So she joined forces with someone who did, Ron MacNeil,
to cofound the Visible Language Workshop at MIT in 1974,
and ran it until her death in 1994. John Maeda, Lisa Strausfeld,
and other influential computer programmers and software
designers were taught by Cooper as she strove to instill the
clarity, ingenuity, wit, and originality that distinguished the
design of her printed books into the otherwise inscrutable
pixelated images on our screens. "Information is only useful,"
she said, "if it can be understood."

HILARY COTTAM

The British social scientist, Hilary Cottam (b. 1965),
founded Participle in 2007 as a social enterprise to prototype
social design projects, which were intended to reinvent
dysfunctional areas of social and health care. During the
1990s Cottam worked for UNICEF and the World Bank as a
specialist in urban poverty. She then experimented with
school and prison design as a founder of School Works and
the Do Tank, before joining the Design Council, the UK's
publicly-funded design champion, in 2001. Six years later,
Cottam cofounded Participle with the aim of redesigning
the welfare state. Participle's work included assisting

the long-term unemployed to return to work, encouraging
disaffected young people to engage with their local
communities, and helping families to emerge from chronic
crises, as well as improving the provision of care for the
elderly. Having developed new approaches to those fields,
Participle's objective was to hand over the long-term
management of the projects to the participants themselves
or to local councils and other suitable organizations. This
policy ensured that many of its projects have flourished
in their new guises since Participle closed in 2015. Cottam
has continued her work in developing new approaches
to social services and health care, and published a book
on her work, *Radical Help*, in 2018.

EMORY DOUGLAS

Born in Grand Rapids, Michigan, Emory Douglas (b. 1943)
grew up in the San Francisco Bay area. After being arrested
in his teens, he was incarcerated in a Youth Training School
in Ontario, California, where he learnt about typography,
layout, and illustration in the print shop. Once released,
Douglas studied graphic design at San Francisco City
College, which was at the heart of the civil rights and anti-
war movements. Flinging himself into activism, he joined
the newly formed Black Panther Party in 1967 and designed
the launch issue of its eponymous newspaper. Douglas
worked on *The Black Panther* in his roles as Revolutionary
Artist and, later, Minister of Culture of the Black Panther
Party, until the paper closed in 1980. Depicting the courage
of the victims of civil rights abuses and the authorities'
brutality against them, Douglas' images were published in
The Black Panther and on fly posters pasted around the party's
base in Oakland. His distinctive graphic style, combining
bold contours and colors in unflinchingly vicious or poignant
images created an instantly recognizable visual identity
for the movement that coined the concept of "radical chic,"
while Douglas himself became a model for younger design
activists. After *The Black Panther* folded, Douglas joined the
San Francisco Sun Reporter, a community newspaper where
he worked for 30 years. Retrospectives of his work opened
at the Museum of Contemporary Art in Los Angeles in 2007
and the New Museum in New York in 2009. His work is

represented in the collection of the National Museum of African American History and Culture in Washington DC, and was featured in the 2017 exhibition *Soul of a Nation: Art in the Age of Black Power* at Tate Modern in London.

CHRISTOPHER DRESSER

At the age of 13, Christopher Dresser (1834–1904) won a place at the Government School of Design in London where the sons of artisans were trained to design for industry. Rather than being taught to draw by depicting the human form as art students were, Dresser and his peers learnt from flowers and plants. After excelling in his studies, Dresser lectured on "artistic botany" during the mid-1850s, while establishing a design studio that developed ceramics, glassware, metalwork, furniture, wallpaper, and textiles, enabling him to study an equally wide range of manufacturing materials and production techniques. Having married at 19, he was under financial pressure to support his growing family, and much of his early work was executed anonymously for the potteries Wedgwood and Minton. Even so, the ambitious, energetic, and personable Dresser was swiftly recognized as an unusually gifted and prolific designer of industrial wares. Throughout his career he forged close relationships with manufacturers that specialized in different techniques, including the silversmiths James Dixon & Sons in Sheffield and Hukin & Heath in Birmingham. In 1879 he joined forces with the entrepreneur John Harrison to open the Linthorpe Art Pottery on Teesside. Linthorpe produced more than 2,000 examples of ceramics, many of them designed by Dresser, in the ten years before it closed. Dresser also continued his research into botany, while pursuing his passion for traditional Japanese craftsmanship. He was the first industrial designer to be widely recognized for imbuing his work with nuance and meaning.

JANE DREW

As one of the few women to enter the male domain of mid-20th-century architecture, Jane Drew (1911–1996) grew accustomed to being described as an architect's wife, rather than a practitioner in her own right. She dealt with such

slights with dignity, and was at pains to champion younger
female architects, including those she hired at the practice
she ran during World War II, initially as a women-only office.
Drew applied the same intelligence, grace, and courage
throughout her working life as a committed modernist in
the conservative culture of British architecture. She completed a succession of ambitious public projects, from
affordable social housing in postwar Britain, to schools
and homes in Ghana and Nigeria. Drew and her husband,
Maxwell Fry (1899–1987), also worked closely with the
Swiss architects Le Corbusier and Pierre Jeanneret on one
of the most ambitious architecture programs of the late
20th century: the design and construction of Chandigarh,
the "City Beautiful," as the capital of the neighboring regions
of Punjab and Haryana in postcolonial India. Together
with Jeanneret, they spent three years working in Chandigarh,
where Le Corbusier visited them during the two coolest
months of each year.

DUNNE & RABY

The British designers Anthony Dunne and Fiona Raby
cofounded Dunne & Raby in London in 1994 as a platform
for their work as designers, teachers, writers, curators,
and design theorists. Not only has their vision of design as
a critical tool of analysis and anticipation inspired their own
students, first at the Royal College of Art in London and,
later, at The New School in New York, it has influenced the
work of the new wave of critical and conceptual designers
worldwide. Dunne and Raby have written extensively
on critical design, and lectured about it internationally.

CHARLES AND RAY EAMES

Charles Eames (1907–1978) was a star design teacher (and
notorious campus lothario) at the Cranbrook Academy of
Art in Michigan in 1940, when he fell in love with an assistant
on one of his projects, Ray Kaiser (1912–1988). They married
the next year, a month after Charles had finalized his divorce
from his first wife, and set off for Los Angeles to build
a new life. Charles supported them financially by designing
sets at MGM's nearby movie studio, and sneaking home

with chunks of plywood and the other materials they needed
to conduct design experiments in their tiny apartment. In
1943 the couple opened a design studio in a decrepit garage
in Venice, where they worked until Charles' death in 1978
and Ray's ten years later. As well as developing furniture and
other products for Herman Miller and other manufacturers,
the Eameses designed modernist houses, including their
own, largely prefabricated home built in a Pacific Palisades
meadow. They also emerged as influential information
designers through the exhibitions and educational films
they made for IBM to raise public awareness and enhance
understanding of the importance of science, mathematics,
and technology.

ECO-FUEL AFRICA

Having decided to design a way of making and selling clean,
affordable cooking fuel to people living in remote, deforested
areas of Africa, the Ugandan design-entrepreneur Sanga
Moses sold almost all of his possessions, including his bed,
to finance the venture. Sanga, who grew up in one of
Uganda's poorest rural regions and was the first member of
his family to go to university, developed a system to convert
organic agricultural waste into charcoal briquettes that
can be used for cooking. Farmers collect organic waste and
convert it into charcoal in kilns provided by Eco-Fuel Africa.
They keep some of the charcoal to fertilize their land,
and sell the rest to the company. Eco-Fuel Africa sells some
charcoal to other farmers as fertilizer, but most of it is
converted into briquettes by local distributors using specially
designed machinery. The briquettes are then delivered
to customers on Eco-Fuel Africa's specially adapted bicycles.
Most of the distributors are women, many of whom are
earning money to support their families for the first time,
and who employ local youths to make deliveries. Since
the first briquettes were sold in 2010, Eco-Fuel Africa has
supplied inexpensive cooking fuel to tens of thousands
of Ugandan homes.

FAIRPHONE

The Dutch social enterprise Fairphone designs smartphones
that are robust, durable, and made on an ethical basis
from responsibly sourced materials, many of them recycled.
Founded in 2013 by the interaction designer and open source
design champion Bas van Abel, and based in Amsterdam,
its mission is "to close the gap between people and their
products … By knowing exactly where stuff comes from and
how it's made, you can make informed decisions about what
you buy." Describing itself as a work in progress, Fairphone
constantly strives to make its phones more ethical, responsible, and sustainable. To this end, the company maps
its supply chain from start to finish, and its business model.
Having refused to use conflict minerals in its products,
Fairphone adopted a policy of sourcing metals and other
materials from former conflict zones with the objective of
helping those regions to rebuild their economies and create
sustainable employment.

STUDIO FORMAFANTASMA

The Italian designers Simone Farresin (b. 1980) and Andrea
Trimarchi (b. 1983) cofounded Studio Formafanstasma
after meeting as students at the Istituto Superiore per le
Industrie Artistiche in Florence. Having applied for a joint
place on the master's course at Design Academy Eindhoven
in the Netherlands only to be told that they had to do so
individually, Farresin and Trimarchi were eventually allowed
to graduate with a collaborative project in 2009. They have
since conducted research projects into design's relationship
with climate change, the rise of racism, the refugee crisis
and migration, rural poverty, Italy's colonial history and
craft traditions, and the often illicit global trade in electronic
and digital waste. Studio Formafantasma remained in
Eindhoven for several years after graduation, then opened
a studio in Amsterdam. Their work has been acquired
for the collections of The Museum of Modern Art, New York,
the Art Institute of Chicago, and the Victoria & Albert
Museum, London. Studio Formafantasma completed its first
industrial project in 2017, a series of lights for the Italian
manufacturer Flos.

R. BUCKMINSTER FULLER

The "simple aim in life'" of the visionary US designer, engineer, and design activist R. Buckminster Fuller (1895–1983) was "to remake the world," claimed *Fortune* magazine in 1946. He did not succeed, but not for the want of trying. Twenty years later, *The New Yorker* billed Fuller as "an engineer, inventor, mathematician, architect, cartographer, philosopher, poet, cosmologist, and comprehensive designer." By then Bucky, as everyone called him, had taken to describing himself as a "comprehensive anticipatory design scientist" and "astronaut from Spaceship Earth." Born into a wealthy New England family, he was among the fifth generation of male Fullers to be admitted to Harvard, and the first not to graduate. His early career was marred by financial crises, yet he continued to pursue his ambition of designing a new form of housing, an affordable living machine (costing no more than a Cadillac) that would be energy-efficient and mass-manufactured for speedy transportation. Fuller's dream was that such a house would heat and cool itself naturally, generate its own power, require minimum maintenance, and could be constantly reconfigured whenever its occupants wished to make it larger or smaller. Bucky devised various versions of the Dymaxion House from the 1920s onward, and adapted the original concept to design Dymaxion Deployment Units, which provided accommodation for the US military in North Africa after World War II. The design formula he developed in the late 1940s to produce an emergency shelter from found materials, the geodesic dome, is one of the most successful humanitarian design projects ever executed.

MARTINO GAMPER

At the age of 14, Martino Gamper (b. 1971) started a five-year apprenticeship with a master craftsman, who made bespoke wooden furniture in his hometown, Merano, in the Italian Tyrol. Realizing that craft was not for him, he studied product design in Vienna. Gamper then worked in Milan for one of his tutors, Matteo Thun, only to chafe against the compromises involved in industrial design, and so decided to work on his own terms as a designer-maker.

After completing a master's degree at the Royal College of
Art in London, he opened a studio where he designed and
made furniture, often using found materials, and conducted
collaborative projects in design and food with friends.
In 2007 Gamper made his name internationally by exhibiting
100 Chairs in 100 Days in London. Each chair was (literally)
made in a day from bits of old furniture he had salvaged
from skips or the streets around his East London studio.
The design historian Emily King described *100 Chairs in 100
Days* as demonstrating "speed, spontaneity, sense of form,
getting better as you go along, and a playful understanding
of design history." Gamper has since established an idiosyncratic and eclectic practice that combines private
commissions and collaborations with artist and designer
friends on exhibitions in art galleries as well as design
spaces, with industrial projects for manufacturers, including
Magis and Moroso. "I'm interested in expressing myself,"
said Gamper, "not thinking about which box I belong to."

AGNES AND RHODA GARRETT

After countless rejections, Agnes Garrett (1845–1935) and
her cousin Rhoda Garrett (1841–1882) finally managed to find
an architect who was willing to take them on as apprentices,
only for him to ban them from entering building sites.
The Garretts accepted, knowing that, as women in the 1870s,
they were very lucky to have found apprenticeships at all.
After completing their training, they set up in business as
"lady decorators" in 1874 with financial support from Agnes'
father, a wealthy corn merchant. In an age when British
homes were dark, fussy, and ornate, the Garretts favoured
a lighter, subtler style for the houses they designed for
fashionable friends and relatives and friends, including the
composer Hubert Parry, and Agnes' sisters, the women's
suffrage campaigner Millicent Fawcett and the pioneering
female doctor Elizabeth Garrett Anderson. The cousins
shared practical tips on how to create "solid and unpreten-
tious interiors" in their 1876 book *Suggestions on House
Decoration*, and answered questions on decoration on
women's suffrage speaking tours. Agnes was so distressed
when Rhoda died of typhoid in 1882, that she considered
closing the business. But she continued, combining

her passions for design and politics by devising housing
or single women as a founding director of the Ladies'
Residential Chambers, before retiring in 1905 to devote
her energy to the women's suffrage campaign.

GRAN FURY

Founded in New York in 1988, Gran Fury was a collective of
activist designer and artists, who were committed to raising
public awareness of AIDS and to correcting the misconceptions and disinformation about it. Named after a model
of car often used for surveillance by the New York Police
Department, Gran Fury was originally part of ACT UP
(the AIDS Coalition to Unleash Power), but soon decided
to operate independently. The group designed posters,
banners, T-shirts, and stickers to educate the public about
the reality of AIDS until its dissolution in 1986. Produced
on a shoestring, its work was incisive, witty, and provocative
with slogans like "Kissing Doesn't Kill: Greed and Indifference Do" and "All People with AIDS Are Innocent."
Some Gran Fury projects were funded by cultural institutions, including the New Museum and Whitney Museum
in New York and the Museum of Contemporary Art in
Los Angeles, but its work was always displayed in public
places, rather than galleries, in the hope of reaching as
broad an audience as possible.

JOOST GROOTENS

In his 2010 book *I Swear I Use No Art at All: 10 Years, 100 Books,
18,788 Pages of Book Design*, Joost Grootens (b. 1971) describes
the process of designing those books not only in words, but
also in maps, charts, grids, and other infographics. The book
includes floor plans of every office and design studio he
has worked in with coded numbers to indicate who sat where.
A map of northern Europe shows the cities where Grootens,
who is based in Amsterdam, has held meetings, printed
books, and staged book launches. He included examples
of every typeface he has used, photographs of the binding
of each book, and coded diagrams of the layouts. There are
also lists of all of the authors, publishers, printers, and
colleagues with whom he has collaborated. Grootens started

out by studying architecture, and worked in multimedia
until a publisher asked him to produce a book version of
a CD-ROM. He taught himself how to do it by scanning and
tracing the pages of books he admired. Grootens has since
specialized in reinventing traditional book typologies,
including the atlas and dictionary, to render them superior
to their digital counterparts. "The quality of the images,
the concentration of information and its materiality are all
characteristics the book has to its advantage over a computer
screen," he has said. "The designer should exploit these
aspects to the fullest."

JING HE

For her graduation project at Design Academy Eindhoven
in 2016, Jing He (b. 1984) investigated the role of copying
in the construction of China's design identity. As an example,
she chose the tulip pyramid, a 17th-century Dutch invention
that imitated the shape, symbolism, and material of Chinese
pagodas. Jing He invited five Chinese designers from
different disciplines to each devise two layers of a new tulip
pyramid. She designed a second pyramid herself by combining her interpretation of well-known examples of Dutch
design with her own work. Born in Kunming in southern
China, Jing He studied jewellery design, first at the Central
Academy of Fine Arts in Beijing, and then at the Gerrit
Rietveld Academy in Amsterdam in the Netherlands, before
completing a master's degree in contextual design at Design
Academy Eindhoven. Since graduating, she has remained
in Eindhoven, working on conceptual and design research
projects.

CHRIS LILJENBERG HALSTRØM

Born in Glostrup, Denmark, to a Swedish mother and
Danish father, Chris Liljenberg Halstrøm (b. 1977) studied
product design in Sweden and Germany before enrolling
at The Royal Danish Academy of Fine Arts in Copenhagen.
After graduating in 2007, Halstrøm opened a design studio
in Copenhagen. Halstrøm combines industrial commissions
for Danish furniture manufacturers including Skagerak,
Frama, and +Halle, with experimental projects. The Georg

collection of wooden furniture designed for Skagerak in 2013 has won many international design awards. Since 2014, Halstrøm has worked with the textile designer Margrethe Odgaard on Included Middle, a collaborative project in which they develop objects that explore the relationship between form, color, and pattern. Halstrøm has defined a disciplined yet sensual design language for products that are gentle and unobtrusive in shape, color, and symbolism, and therefore open to interpretation by each individual who encounters them.

CHARLES HARRISON

One of the most prolific US consumer product designers of the late 20ᵗʰ century, Charles Harrison (b. 1931) overcame prejudice and oppression to forge a successful career and to become the first African-American winner of the Lifetime Achievement National Design Award in 2008. Born in Shreveport, Louisiana, Harrison was introduced to design by his father, an industrial arts professor. Another important early influence was his maternal grandfather, who, like Harrison's father, loved carpentry. Harrison studied design at the School of the Art Institute of Chicago and the Illinois Institute of Technology, before working for commercial design consultancies in Chicago, where he completed several assignments for the Sears, Roebuck retail group. Sears offered him a job in 1961, and Harrison became the first African-American executive to work at its Chicago headquarters. He had applied to Sears several years before only to be rebuffed because of its unwritten policy against hiring African-Americans. In over 30 years as head of design at Sears, Harrison was involved in the development of more than 600 products, including hair dryers, hedge clippers, power tools, toasters, lawn mowers, wheelbarrows, and the first plastic trash can. After leaving Sears in 1993, Harrison taught design at the University of Illinois and the School of the Art Institute of Chicago. He favored a utilitarian approach to design throughout his career."If it doesn't do what it's supposed to do, or look like what it does, then I frown on it," he said, "I don't think a nutcracker needs to look like an elephant."

HELLA JONGERIUS

After leaving high school in the Dutch village of De Meern, Hella Jongerius (b. 1963) enrolled on a carpentry course and then studied product design at Design Academy Eindhoven. She graduated in 1993 and set up a studio in Rotterdam, exhibiting her work with that of other young Dutch designers in the Droog Design group. Jongerius experimented with ways of imbuing mass-manufactured objects with the subtlety, idiosyncrasy, and warmth that people relish in craftsmanship. Often she used artisanal references to imply that an object was handmade by adding tiny imperfections that are typical of antiques or hand-crafted pots. Jongerius achieved similar effects by creating unusual combinations of vibrant colors and bold textures. She moved her studio from Rotterdam to Berlin in 2008. Many of her early projects were self-funded limited editions, but Jongerius has subsequently worked on an industrial scale for global brands including the IKEA retail group, the Dutch airline KLM, the US textile company Maharam, and the Swiss furniture manufacturer Vitra, for which she has conducted a long-term study into materials and color. Jongerius also collaborated with the Dutch design critic Louise Schouwenberg on *Beyond the New*, a campaign to encourage designers to be more responsible in their use of natural resources. As Jongerius put it: "There's too much shit design."

DIÉBÉDO FRANCIS KÉRÉ

As a child, the Burkinabé architect Diébédo Francis Kéré (b. 1965) traveled nearly 25 miles to attend the nearest school to Gando, the village where he was born. When Kéré left Burkina Faso to study architecture in Berlin, becoming the first person from Gando to be educated in another country, he was given coins by elderly villagers as tokens that, they believed, would persuade him to return and help the local community. Convinced that the village needed a good school, he set about raising the funds to design and build one. As well as persuading his Berlin friends to support the project, Kéré secured a grant from the Burkinabé government to train local people to make the school's walls and ceilings from compressed clay found locally. Every element of the structure was designed to protect the students from Gando's brutal climate by sheltering them from the extremes of strong sunlight and torrential rains, and making the interior as cool as possible. The school was completed in 2001, and has proved so effective that Kéré, who is based in Berlin, has expanded it and designed more educational buildings in the village. He has also worked on architectural projects in other areas of Burkina Faso, as well as in Mali, Yemen, China, Switzerland, and the United Kingdom, where he designed a summer pavilion for the Serpentine Galleries in London in 2017.

MAX LAMB

The British designer Max Lamb (b. 1980) combines advanced technologies with craft techniques to develop furniture and other objects that are inspired by his childhood memories of the countryside and rural craftsmanship. Lamb's work is defined by his fascination with materials and the stories behind them. He transformed a dead 187-year-old female ash tree from his grandfather's farm in north Yorkshire into 131 log seats, tables, and benches. The formula for a new man-made marble was made by combining four different types of marble, each with a rich history, extracted from mines near Verona in northern Italy. The Crockery collection of plates, bowls, cups, jugs, and vases that Lamb designed for the British ceramics manufacturer 1882 Ltd, was inspired by the white stream of liquefied clay that ran past his childhood home in Cornwall during heavy rain. Crockery is made partly from the same type of clay, using molds of models Lamb constructed by bashing solid blocks of plaster with a stone mason's chisel to ensure that the surfaces look so strange and staccato that each identical object of the same type appears unique.

GABRIEL A. MAHER

Gender politics is the focus of Gabriel A. Maher's work in design research, and in conceptual and performative design projects. As well as exploring the influence of the design industry and media on our perceptions of gender, Maher (b. 1983) has investigated the possibility of more fluid and

expressive alternatives in a series of DE_SIGN projects.
Born in Sydney, Australia, Maher studied interior architecture
and design at the University of New South Wales before
teaching and practicing in Sydney and Melbourne. Maher
moved to the Netherlands in 2012 to study for a master's
degree in social design at Design Academy Eindhoven.
Maher graduated in 2014 with a research project that analyzed
the presentation of gender in a year of issues of the Dutch
design magazine *Frame*. Since then, Maher has lectured and
staged performances worldwide, and completed an Iaspis
residency, organized by the Swedish Arts Grants Committee,
in Stockholm, Sweden during 2016 and 2017.

CHRISTIEN MEINDERTSMA

Buying, categorizing, and recording a week's worth of
objects (3,267 of them) confiscated during security checks
at Schiphol Airport in Amsterdam following the 9/11 terrorist
attacks was Christien Meindertsma's first design project.
Since completing it in 2004, a year after she graduated from
Design Academy Eindhoven in the Netherlands,
Meindertsma (b. 1980) has applied a similarly rigorous
research process to the flax harvest of a Dutch farm, one
woman's knitting output, the prairie plants growing in the
Nachusa Grasslands in Illinois, the contents of a pig, and
whatever was left of the roadkill carcasses in a Dutch nature
reserve after scavengers had preyed on them. All of her
work flushes out unexpected discoveries and insights.
Meindertsma also strives to produce useful things from stuff
that is typically written off as damaged, defunct, or valueless.
She made a chair from the flax, and exquisitely colored
papers from the prairie plants. The pig's parts sparked an
eloquent exposé of the ambiguity and hypocrisy of food and
farming politics, while the roadkill remains were reinvented
as an elegant set of bone china objects.

MEMPHIS

On the evening of December 11, 1980, the 61-year-old Ettore
Sottsass gathered a group of younger designers to his Milan
apartment, and invited them to collaborate on a collection
of furniture to be exhibited at the 1981 Milan Furniture Fair.

It was to be a protest against the ascetic modernist style that had defined industrial design for decades. They adopted the name Memphis for the group because Bob Dylan's *Stuck Inside of Mobile* was on the record player that night, and the needle got stuck on the words "Memphis Blues Again." The furniture they designed was flamboyant, colorful, and gleefully kitsch. Conceptually, Memphis was far from innovative: most of the ideas had been developed in the 1970s by Radical Design groups like Studio Alchimia, on which Sottsass had collaborated with his friend Alessandro Mendini. But Memphis was more visible, thanks to Sottsass' flair for marketing. There were long lines of people waiting outside the opening of the debut exhibition during the Milan fair. Photographs of Sottsass posing with his young collaborators in a "conversation pit" devised by the Japanese designer Masanori Umeda to resemble a boxing ring, were printed in design magazines worldwide. Showy and media-savvy, Memphis presented fashionable, but often inscrutable postmodernist design theory in an accessible guise as design's equivalent of Ronald Reagan's photo-opp' presidency, and the pantaloon-clad New Romantics who preened in early MTV promos. But there was only so much leopard-printed plastic laminate that Sottsass could take and in 1985 he quit Memphis, followed, eventually, by most of his young collaborators.

ALESSANDRO MENDINI

The Italian product designer and architect Alessandro Mendini (b. 1931) was born to a wealthy Milanese family, and studied architecture at Milan Polytechnic. After graduating he worked in the architectural studio of Marcello Nizzoli, who was chief design consultant to Olivetti, the Italian electronics company which he had established as a model of modern corporate design. By the late 1960s Mendini had become immersed in Italy's Radical Design movement in which groups such as Archizoom and Superstudio treated design as a conceptual tool to challenge the establishment by developing utopian projects. Having championed Radical Design as editor of the design journal *Casabella* in the early 1970s, Mendini did the same for postmodernism as editor-in-chief of *Domus* in the late 1970s and early 1980s. During this

period he continued to design politically-charged conceptual projects, for example, by filming the destruction by fire
of his archetypal 1974 wooden chair Lassù. Mendini left
Domus in 1985 to build up his architecture practice with his
younger brother Francesco (b. 1939), notably by leading a
group of international architects who collaborated on the
design of the Groninger Museum in the Netherlands.

MIGRATIONLAB

Founded in 2014 by the Romanian social designer Laura
Pana, Migrationlab started out as a blog that shared the
stories of refugees and migrants trying to build new lives in
new countries. A year later Pana reinvented it as a nonprofit
organization that creates safe, welcoming spaces in different
European cities, where migrants and asylum seekers can
meet people from their new communities, including those
who may feel disconcerted by their arrival. Pana was inspired
by her own experience of traveling across Europe as a
migrant from Romania at the age of 26, first to Vienna, and
then to The Hague. (She returned to Vienna in 2017.)
Her objective is to help other migrants to settle into their
new communities by enabling them to share insights and
information with local people, and to receive practical
advice and support.

LÁSZLÓ MOHOLY-NAGY

One of the most dynamic designers and visual theorists
of the early 20th century, László Moholy-Nagy (1895–1946)
was born to a well-connected but cash-strapped Jewish
family in Bácsborsód in southern Hungary. After fighting in
the Hungarian army during World War I he studied art in
Budapest and joined the constructivist groups that were then
emerging in the city. Moholy-Nagy left Hungary in 1919
to live in Vienna and then in Berlin, where he established
himself as a charismatic avant-garde artist and visual theorist. He continued to experiment with new media, including
photography and film as a teacher at the Bauhaus in the
mid-1920s, during his brief exiles in the Netherlands and
Britain, and at the two design schools he set up in Chicago
after moving to the United States with his family in 1937.

Prolific as well as innovative Moholy-Nagy produced a vast and eclectic body of work, including drawings, paintings, photography, films, stage sets, graphic design, sculpture, and industrial design, as well as writing a constant stream of essays and books, culminating in *Vision in Motion*, published a year after his death. Long praised for pioneering film and photography, as well as for working across diverse creative disciplines, Moholy-Nagy is increasingly recognized as an important early influence on the design of digital imagery.

CARLO MOLLINO

The gifted mid-20th-century Italian furniture designer Carlo Mollino (1905–1973) distanced himself from the Milanese design establishment by living and working in his birthplace, Turin. A complex, often contrary character, Mollino was described by his father, a wealthy industrialist, as a "feckless good-for-nothing," and by a university friend as "diabolic." He played up to his reputation as the "dark prince of Italian design" by cultivating an air of mystery and styling himself as a mustachioed pantomime villain. So many myths have surfaced about Mollino since his sudden death in 1973 that it is difficult to distinguish fact from fiction. Did he really sleep all day and work all night? Race a car he had designed himself at Le Mans? Insist that his furniture was only ever made on Sundays, when no one would see it in the workshops? Crash his airplane into a high voltage cable, and walk away from the wreckage unscathed? Mollino was as gifted and disciplined as he was decadent, and the architecture, interiors, and objects he designed in his native Turin were original and ingenious, and remained hugely influential.

HANS MONDERMAN

Born in Leeuwarden in the northern Netherlands, Hans Monderman (1945–2008) started out as a civil engineer, but rapidly became as interested in how people respond to roads as he was in building them. To better understand the psychology of road users, Monderman trained as an advanced driving instructor and worked as an accident investigator. In 1979, he found a role that combined all of his interests by becoming a traffic safety consultant for the region of Friesland. During the 1980s and 1990s, Monderman conducted a series of radical experiments on the roads of towns and villages in Friesland. He stripped them of signs and other traffic controls in the belief that if drivers and pedestrians feel confused, they are likely to behave more cautiously. Monderman's "naked" or "shared streets" have since been implemented by towns and cities worldwide.

THE OCEAN CLEANUP

The plastic debris cluttering the oceans is one of our biggest pollution problems, particularly in the northern Pacific where plastic represents the bulk of the Great Garbage Patch, which has accumulated there and is now larger in size than Texas. Based in Delft in the Netherlands, the Ocean Cleanup was founded in 2013 by Boyan Slat (b. 1994), who formulated the concept while studying aerospace engineering there. Slat mounted an impassioned crowdfunding campaign to secure the capital required to complete the prototyping and initial tests of a giant floating structure with which he intended to collect and contain plastic trash before removing it from the water for responsible recycling and disposal on dry land. He succeeded in raising $2.2 million from 38,000 donors in 160 countries in 2014, and assembled a team of designers, scientists, engineers, and other specialists to refine the technology. Despite criticism from scientists and ecologists, the Ocean Cleanup tested its floating structure off the Dutch coast in the North Sea, and announced in spring 2017 that it had raised an additional $22m in donations, taking the total to $31.5 million. The Ocean Cleanup then conducted large-scale tests of its system in the Pacific before deploying it in 2018 with the aim of clearing half of the Great Garbage Patch within five years.

VICTOR PAPANEK

Born in "Red Vienna," Victor Papanek (1923–1998) was educated in England before moving to the United States in 1939 to escape World War II. After attending the architectural school run by his design hero, Frank Lloyd Wright, at Taliesin West in Arizona, Papanek studied architecture and design at the Cooper Union in New York and enrolled on a creative engineering course at the Massachusetts Institute of Technology. Having tried—and loathed—working in commercial design, he pursued a career in teaching and design research, conducting anthropological projects while living among the Navajos, Inuits, and other indigenous communities. Papanek distilled his observations into his 1971 book, *Design for the Real World: Human Ecology and Social Change*, which expresses his vision of humane and sustainable design. Filled with references to Hermann Hesse, Arthur Koestler, the postindustrial housing at the Drop City commune in Colorado, and a Californian farm powered by the manure of its pigs, *Design for the Real World* is one of the best-selling books ever to have been published on design.

PEEK VISION

Four out of five of the 285 million people with impaired vision worldwide could regain their sight if they were treated correctly, according to the World Health Organization. The problem is that most of these people live in countries where the necessary medical specialists and equipment are scarce. Peek Vision, a group of doctors and designers in Kenya, have devised a solution in Peek Retina, a smart phone adaptor and app, which produces such high quality images of the retina that cataracts, glaucoma, and other problems can be swiftly identified even in remote locations hundreds of miles from specialist facilities. If problems are spotted, the patients can be referred for treatment, and, if expert analysis is required, their data can be sent online to the relevant specialists. Peek Retina is easier to use and considerably cheaper than a traditional ophthalmoscope which means that nurses, general practitioners, and even medical students can make diagnoses with it. In a country like Kenya, where more than 80% of adults have access to cell phones, ingenious Internet of Things devices like Peek Retina promise to improve the health of millions of people.

CHARLOTTE PERRIAND

The French designer and architect Charlotte Perriand (1903–1999) was a resourceful and resilient character, who made an important contribution to modernism, while pursuing her social and political concerns. As both her parents were skilled workers for Parisian couture houses, she grew up surrounded by artisans, and studied interior design at the Union Centrale des Arts Décoratifs. Perriand then joined Le Corbusier's studio in Paris, where she designed furniture for his buildings. At that time, she favored a glacially elegant, technocratic style of design, but from the late 1930s Perriand experimented with applying modernist principles to the rustic materials and symbolism of Savoie, the Alpine region where her grandparents lived. Her organic take on modernism was enhanced by her study of traditional Asian craftsmanship when she found herself stranded in Japan and Vietnam during Word War II. Back in France after the war, Perriand established herself as an architect through commissions for Air France and other corporate clients, as well as a project to design a new ski resort at Méribel in her beloved Savoie.

FRANK PICK

It seems apt that one of the best loved symbols of London, the ingenious diagrammatic map of the London Underground designed by the draughtsman Harry Beck, was introduced in 1933, the same year that Frank Pick became managing director of the newly formed London Passenger Transport Board. A lawyer by training, Pick (1878–1941) joined the London Underground in 1906 as an assistant to the deputy chairman. While working his way up the ranks, he developed an unusually sophisticated understanding of the importance of design in defining the network's identity. Thanks to his influence, artists such as Man Ray, Graham Sutherland, Edward McKnight Kauffer, and Paul Nash were commissioned to design posters, as was László Moholy-Nagy. Pick also helped to ensure that Edward Johnston designed the London Underground's typeface and its famous red, white, and blue "bull's eye" roundel symbol. Critically, Pick realized that, if his inspired design commissions were to be effective, they had to be scrupulously maintained. He devoted evenings and weekends until his retirement in 1940 to traveling the length of the network, checking that everything was up to scratch. Pick made a note of any glitches, and fired off memos the next

day, instructing depot and station managers to remove
peeling posters or to mend fraying upholstery.

EMILY PILLOTON

After starting Project H in 2008 from her laptop on the
dining table in her parents' home in Kentfield, California,
with $1,000 of savings, the US designer Emily Pilloton
(b. 1981) established it as an international network of
humanitarian designers. Eager to return to grassroots
activism, she cofounded Studio H as an experimental high
school design course. Studio H aims to equip kids with
design and making skills as lifelong resources to help them
to become more confident, resourceful, and imaginative.
Pilloton went on to develop Girls Garage as a series of
summer and after-school workshops that teach design
and building techniques to girls aged from nine to 17.
Encompassing design, electronics, carpentry, architecture,
engineering, welding, fix-it, and leadership, the workshops
are intended to "build confidence, grit, and the belief that
everything is possible in life and the world." Every camp
graduate is given a Fearless Builder Girl certificate. The
program's motto is "Fuse metal. Make trouble. Speak up.
Stand out." In 2015 Pilloton launched the Unprofessional
Development program to help teachers to learn how to teach
design, making, and building skills.

CLARA PORSET

Despite being thrown out of her native Cuba not one or two,
but three times, Clara Porset (1895–1981) became one of
the most influential 20th-century furniture designers there,
and in her adopted country, Mexico. Born to a wealthy
Cuban family, Porset studied in New York and Paris before
returning to her homeland in 1932, only to be expelled
because of her radical politics. She was ejected again three
years later, and fled to Mexico with her lover, the artist and
activist Xavier Guerrero. They traveled around the country
visiting craft workshops and researching Mexico's artisanal
heritage. Porset defined a singular design language by
infusing modernist efficiency with the sensual qualities she
loved in Mexican craft culture in the furniture she designed

for Luis Barragán, Enrique Yáñez, and other architects. Her 1952 exhibition *Art in Daily Life* at the Palacio de Bellas Artes in Mexico City combined industrial and artisanal artifacts in a manifesto for her belief that craft and industry could be mutually enriching. Porset's success in Mexico prompted Fidel Castro to invite her back to Cuba after he took power in 1959 to open a design school. But she and Guerrero returned to Mexico in 1963 after falling out with their colleagues at the school and with the Castro regime.

POTTERS FOR PEACE

One of the most efficient ways of helping the billion-plus people worldwide without access to clean, safe water is the Ceramic Water Filter Project run by the US-based nonprofit Potters for Peace. The design template for a water filter made in the shape of a bucket from local terracotta mixed with sawdust or rice husks was devised by the Guatemalan designer and chemist Fernando Mazariegos, in 1981. The filters are fired at such high temperatures that the clay becomes porous enough for water to pass through, leaving any dirt behind. In 1998, when members of Potters for Peace were trying to help the victims of Hurricane Mitch in Central America, they discovered Mazariegos's filters. Potters for Peace set up a workshop in Nicaragua, which produced over 5,000 filters in six months. Having decided that the most efficient way of increasing production would be to train local communities to make the filters themselves, they began a long-term program to do so. It has since helped to establish workshops in dozens of countries and has distributed hundreds of thousands of filters to people in urgent need of clean water.

JEAN PROUVÉ

The French designer, architect, and manufacturer Jean Prouvé (1901–1984) was passionately committed to the modernist ideal of deploying design and technology to improve the lives of the masses. Born in Paris, he grew up in Nancy, where his father, Victor, cofounded the École de Nancy, a group of local artists, artisans, and industrialists who championed Art Nouveau. After being apprenticed to master blacksmiths in Paris, Prouvé opened a forge in Nancy in 1923, making wrought iron grilles and doors, and later furniture and other architectural components for schools, factories, and hospitals. Adopting an uncompromisingly utilitarian approach to design, Prouvé developed each piece to fulfill its function using minimal materials. During World War II he joined the French Resistance, and began the research into designing prefabricated structures for speedy assembly that he applied to emergency housing after the war. Prouvé designed more sophisticated forms of prefabrication in the factory he opened in Nancy in 1947, only to be forced out of it five years later by his financial backer. "If people understand, there's no need to explain," he wrote. "If they don't, there's no use explaining."

DIETER RAMS

In over 30 years as chief design officer of the German electronics company Braun, Dieter Rams (b. 1932) defined an intelligent, empathic, and efficient design language that helped postwar consumers to engage with the hitherto daunting world of electronics. Rams' work at Braun has served as a model of modern design ever since. Born in Wiesbaden, he studied architecture and interior design at the local art school. After graduating in 1953, Rams joined the office of a Frankfurt architect. In 1955 he and his colleagues spotted a job ad in a local newspaper for an in-house architect at Braun, and they dared one another to apply. Rams got it. Having started out at Braun by designing exhibition sets, he diversified into product design. The firstproduct he worked on from start to finish was the SK4, a 1956 record player and radio whose glacial aesthetic prompted its nickname "Snow White's Coffin." As well as the hundreds of products he developed at Braun, Rams has designed modular furniture systems, including storage, seating, desks, and tables that can be configured to suit each user for the manufacturer Vitsoe.

LILLY REICH

By the time she met the architect Mies van der Rohe in 1926, Lilly Reich (1885–1947) was established as one of Germany's most innovative interior designers, and the first woman to have joined the governing board of the Deutscher Werkbund. She and Mies became lovers, but maintained their own studios while collaborating on exhibitions of housing, construction, and clothing, as well as on the design of the furniture and interiors of Mies' buildings, including the Barcelona Pavilion and Villa Brno. Two years after Mies became director of the Bauhaus in 1930, he appointed Reich as head of the weaving and interiors workshops. She managed much of the school's administration until the Nazis closed it in 1933. Mies fled to exile in the United States, where he became one of the most eminent architects of the postwar era. Reich suffered severely from the hardship of life in wartime Germany, and died two years after the war ended. Thanks to her courage and foresight, the archives of Mies's prewar work, as well as her own, survived the war intact, and are now part of the collection of The Museum of Modern Art in New York. The extent of Reich's influence on Mies' architecture is unclear, but the interiors of his postwar buildings, in particular, were seldom as refined and sensual as those designed in collaboration with her.

WILLEM SANDBERG

The Dutch curator and graphic designer Willem Sandberg (1897–1984) was born to a wealthy family in Amersfoort. He studied art in Amsterdam, before traveling around Europe for several years, spending time at the Bauhaus and working at a Swiss print shop where he became fascinated by typography. Back in Amsterdam, Sandberg opened a graphic design studio, working mostly for the Stedelijk Museum, which eventually appointed him as a curator. During the German Occupation of the Netherlands in World War II Sandberg joined the Dutch Resistance, and was forced to go into hiding for the final 15 months of the war. When peace was declared he returned to Amsterdam, where he was appointed director of the Stedelijk, and insisted on combining his directorial duties with designing all of the museum's graphics. After retiring from the Stedelijk in 1962, Sandberg continued to execute design projects, including the visual identity of the newly founded Israel Museum in Jerusalem, and a set of Dutch stamps.

SEHAT KAHANI

The Pakistani doctors Sara Khurram and Iffat Zafar cofounded DoctHERS in Karachi in 2014 with the social entrepreneur Asher Hasan as a digital medical platform through which female patients could be treated remotely by women doctors. They worked together to establish a network of teleclinics until 2017, when Khurram and Zafar decided to work independently from Hasan. They started a new venture, Sehat Zahani, which means "Story of Health" in Urdu, to manage and expand the teleclinic network that they had originally established for DoctHERS.

ETTORE SOTTSASS JR.

The architect and designer Ettore Sottsass Jr. (1917–2007), was born in Innsbruck to an Austrian mother and Italian father (also named Ettore, and also an architect). Sottsass grew up in Turin, where he studied architecture at university. After graduating in 1939, he served in the Italian army during World War II, only to be captured and incarcerated in a concentration camp near Sarajevo. Back in Italy, he worked for his father for a year before opening his own design studio in Milan in 1946. Sottsass made ends meet by designing exhibition sets, trade fair stands, and occasional pieces of furniture, while engaging in design discourse by writing for the art and architecture journal *Domus*. In 1956 he and his wife, the writer Fernanda Pivano, flew to New York, where Sottsass had been offered a month of paid work with the industrial designer George Nelson. Shortly after their return to Italy, Sottsass began a long and fruitful collaboration with the office equipment company Olivetti, which established him as a force on the Italian design scene. As well as designing mass-manufactured products for Olivetti, Poltronova, and Alessi, Sottsass collaborated with Italian artisans on smaller editions of ceramics and glassware. Even so, he is best known for popularizing postmodernism as the leader of the Memphis group, which he founded in Milan in 1980.

GUNTA STÖLZL

Born in Munich, Gunta Stölzl (1897–1983) studied glass
painting and ceramics at the city's School of Applied Arts,
which was run by Richard Riemerschmid, a progressive
architect, who encouraged her to experiment. During World
War I Stölzl volunteered as a Red Cross nurse on the French
and Italian fronts before resuming her studies in Munich,
only to subsequently enroll at a new, reputedly more radical
school, the Bauhaus. She was assigned to the "women's
class" to study textiles, where she experimented with new
approaches to dyes, finishes, and embellishment, and
developed synthetic fibers. Stölzl also devised innovative
ways of testing textiles for their strength, light resistance,
and durability. As a teacher at the Bauhaus, she encouraged
her students to do the same. Having lost her German
citizenship by marrying a fellow Bauhaüsler, the Palestinian
architect Arieh Sharon, Stölzl became vulnerable to Nazi
persecution, and was dismissed from the Bauhaus in 1931.
She left Germany that year for Switzerland with their
daughter Yael, while Sharon returned to Palestine. They
divorced five years later. In Switzerland Stölzl rebuilt her
career by undertaking large weaving commissions, and
cofounded several textile mills, including Hand Weaving
Studio Flora.

VITRA CAMPUS

The construction of the Vitra Campus began with a catastro-
phe when the original furniture factories and warehouses
on the site near Weil-am-Rhein on the Swiss-German border
were destroyed by fire in 1981. Vitra's then-chairman Rolf
Fehlbaum commissioned the British architect Nicholas
Grimshaw to design two new factories to replace them. After
meeting the US architect Frank Gehry, Fehlbaum invited
him to design a third factory and a small museum to house
Vitra's rapidly expanding collection of modern and contemporary furniture. Vitra went on to realize Zaha Hadid's
first building, a fire station completed in 1993, and to give
Tadao Ando his first European project, a conference center.
Subsequent additions to the company's architecture
collection include: SANAA's first industrial building, and

two projects by Herzog & de Meuron, the Vitra Haus and the Schaudepot archive and curatorial research center. Visits to the site have increased steadily, and the Vitra Design Museum now conducts five guided tours of the complex every day.

SŌETSU YANAGI

As a cofounder of the *mingei* Japanese folk-craft movement in the 1930s, the philosopher and cultural historian Sōetsu Yanagi (1889–1961) played an important part in developing a modern approach to Japanese design, rooted in the aesthetics and values of the country's artisanal traditions. Born into a wealthy Tokyo family, Yanagi was obsessed by Western philosophy, science, and culture in his 20s, and became equally enthralled by historic Japanese and Korean art and craftsmanship, particularly the "folk-craftwork" made by rural artisans. Through his lectures and writing Yanagi championed the purity and modesty of the folk-crafts as an alternative to what he saw as the brutality of industrialization. Eloquent and charismatic, he exercised considerable influence over artists and intellectuals in Japan and other countries through his friendships with the British potter Bernard Leach, the US-Japanese sculptor Isamu Noguchi, the German architect Bruno Taut, and eventually his son, Sori.

SORI YANAGI

Born in Tokyo, Sori Yanagi (1915–2011) was a teenager when his father, Sōetsu, cofounded the *mingei* movement to champion the virtues of Japan's folkloric and craft traditions. Sōetsu was at the heart of the Japanese cultural scene, and introduced his son to a succession of Japanese and Western artists, architects, and designers. While Sori was studying art and architecture in Tokyo in the early 1940s, he worked as a translator for the French designer Charlotte Perriand, who introduced him to product design. During the postwar years, Yanagi emerged as one of Japan's most influential and prolific industrial designers by fusing the traditional qualities of simplicity, strength, and subtlety that his father cherished in *mingei*, with Perriand's technocratic vision of modernity. He designed a remarkable range of objects, frommanhole covers to soy sauce pots and the official torch for the 1972 Sapporo Winter Olympics. His products are still used daily in millions of Japanese homes.

Bibliography

All websites cited in the notes were accessed and verified in May 2018.

Stanley Abercrombie, *George Nelson: The Design of Modern Design* (1995), The MIT Press, Cambridge, Massachusetts 2000.

Annmarie Adams, *Architecture in the Family Way: Doctors, Houses and Women, 1870–1900*, McGill-Queen's University Press, Montreal, Quebec and Kingston, Ontario 2001.

Glenn Adamson, Jane Pavitt (ed.), *Postmodernism: Style and Subversion, 1970–1990*, exh. cat., V&A Publishing Ltd, London 2011.

Anni Albers, *On Weaving* (1965), Princeton University Press, Princeton, New Jersey and Woodstock, New York 2017.

Ed Annink, Max Bruinsma (eds.), *Gerd Arntz: Graphic Designer*, 010 Publishers, Rotterdam 2010.

Paola Antonelli (ed.), *Design and the Elastic Mind*, The Museum of Modern Art, New York 2008.

Paola Antonelli, Jamer Hunt (eds.), *Design and Violence*, The Museum of Modern Art, New York 2015.

Paola Antonelli, *Humble Masterpieces: 100 Everyday Marvels of Design* (2005), Thames & Hudson, London 2006.

Paola Antonelli, Michelle Fisher (eds.), *Items: Is Fashion Modern?* The Museum of Modern Art, New York 2017.

Paola Antonelli (ed.), *Safe: Design Takes on Risk*, The Museum of Modern Art, New York 2006.

Paola Antonelli (ed.), *Talk To Me: Design and Communication between People and Objects*, The Museum of Modern Art, New York 2011.

Marie J. Aquilino (ed.), *Beyond Shelter: Architecture and Human Dignity*, Metropolis Books, New York 2011.

Judy Attfield, Pat Kirkham (eds.), *A View from the Interior: Feminism, Women and Design*, The Women's Press, London 1989.

Phil Baines, *Penguin by Design: A Cover Story 1935–2005*, Allen Lane, London 2005.

Reyner Banham, *Theory and Design in The First Machine Age* (1960), Butterworth Architecture, Oxford 1992.

Stephen Banham, *Characters: Cultural Stories Revealed through Typography*, Thames & Hudson, London 2011.

Roland Barthes, *The Fashion System* (1967), University of California Press, Berkeley, California 1990.

Roland Barthes, *Mythologies* (1957), Paladin, Frogmore 1973.

Jennifer Bass, Pat Kirkham, *Saul Bass: A Life in Film & Design*, Laurence King Publishing, London 2011.

Jean Baudrillard, *The System of Objects* (1968), Verso, London 2005.

Bauhaus-Archiv Berlin, Stiftung Bauhaus Dessau, Klassik Stiftung Weimar, *Bauhaus: A Conceptual Model*, Hatje Cantz Verlag, Ostfildern-Ruit 2009.

Herbert Bayer, Ise Gropius, Walter Gropius (eds.), *Bauhaus 1919–1928*, The Museum of Modern Art, New York 1938.

Honor Beddard, Douglas Dodds, *Digital Pioneers*, V&A Publishing, London 2009.

Marshall Berman, *All That Is Solid Melts Into Air: The Experience of Modernity*, Verso, London 1990.

Anthony Bertram, *Design*, Penguin, Harmondsworth 1938.

Regina Lee Blaszczyk, *The Color Revolution*, The MIT Press, Cambridge, Massachusetts 2012.

Andrew Blauvelt, Ellen Lupton (eds.), *Graphic Design: Now in Production*, Walker Art Center, Minneapolis, Minnesota 2011.

Florian Böhm (ed.), *KGID Konstantin Grcic Industrial Design*, Phaidon Press, London 2005.

Olivier Boissière, *StarckÒ*, Taschen, Cologne 1991.

Irma Boom (ed.), *Irma Boom: Biography in Books, Books in Reverse Chronological Order 2010–1986*, University of Amsterdam Press, Amsterdam 2010.

Irma Boom (ed.), *Irma Boom: The Architecture of the Book, Books in Reverse chronological order 2013–1986*, Lecturis, Eindhoven 2013.

Irma Boom (ed.), *Présent*, Renault, Boulogne-Billancourt 2016.

Achim Borchardt-Hume (ed.), *Albers and Moholy-Nagy: From the Bauhaus to the New World*, exh. cat., Tate Publishing, London 2006.

Ralph Borland, Michael John Gorman, Bruce Misstear, Jane Withers, *Surface Tension: The Future of Water*, Science Gallery, Dublin 2011.

Ronan Bouroullec, Erwan Bouroullec (eds.), *Ronan and Erwan Bouroullec*, Phaidon Press, London 2003.

Nicolas Bourriaud, *Relational Aesthetics*, Les Presses du réel, Dijon 1998.

Charles Arthur Boyer, Federica Zanco, *Jasper Morrison*, Éditions dis Voir, Paris 1999.

Kim Brandt, *Kingdom of Beauty: Mingei and the Politics of Folk Art in Imperial Japan*, Duke University Press, Durham, North Carolina 2007.

Michael Braungart, William McDonough, *Cradle to Cradle: Re-Making the Way we Make Things* (2002), Jonathan Cape, London 2008.

Christopher Breward, Ghislaine Wood (eds.), *British Design from 1948: Innovation in the Modern Age*, exh. cat., V&A Publishing, London 2012.

Giovanni Brino, *Carlo Mollino: Architecture as Autobiography*, Thames & Hudson, London 1987.

Jacob Bromberg, Michael Connor, Clara Meister, Kristina Scepanski (eds.), *Elephant Child: Camille Henrot*, Inventory Press/Koenig Books, New York/London 2016.

Rita Brons, Bernard Colenbrander (eds.), *New Dutch Water Defence Line*, 010 Publishers, Amsterdam 2009.

Charlotte Brontë, *The Letters of Charlotte Brontë: With a Selection of Letters by Family and Friends: Volume Two, 1848–1851*, Oxford University Press, Oxford 2000.

Jerry Brotton, *A History of the World in Twelve Maps*, Allen Lane, London 2012.

Tim Brown, *Change by Design: How Design Thinking Transforms Organizations and Inspires Innovation* HarperCollins Publishers, New York 2009.

Cheryl Buckley, *Potters and Paintesses: Women Designers in the Pottery Industry 1870–1955*, The Women's Press, London 1990.

R. Buckminster Fuller, *Operating Manual for Spaceship Earth*, Southern Illinois University Press, Carbondale, Illinois 1969.

Peter Burke, *The Fabrication of Louis XIV*, Yale University Press, New Haven, Connecticut 1992.

Jason T. Busch, Catherine L. Futter (eds.), *Inventing the Modern World: Decorative Arts at the World's Fairs 1851–1939*, Skira Rizzoli International Publications, New York 2012.

Martha Buskirk, Mignon Nixon (eds.), *The Duchamp Effect: Essays, Interviews, Round Table*, The MIT Press Cambridge, Massachusetts 1996.

Vincent Catz (ed.), *Black Mountain College: Experiment in Art*, The MIT Press, Cambridge, Massachusetts 2013.

Germano Celant (ed.), *Espressioni di Gio Ponti*, Electa, Milan 2011.

C. J. Chivers, *The Gun: The AK-47 and the Evolution of War*, Allen Lane, London 2010.

Deborah Cohen, *Household Gods: The British and their Possessions*, Yale University Press, New Haven, Connecticut 2006.

Alex Coles (ed.), *EP/Volume. 2: Design Fiction*, Sternberg Press, Berlin 2016.

Beatriz Colomina, Mark Wigley, *are we human? notes on an archaeology of design* Lars Müller Publishers, Zurich 2016.

Mariana Cook, *Stone Walls: Personal Boundaries*, Damiani Editore, Bologna 2011.

Peter Cook (ed.), *A Guide to Archigram 1961–1974*, Academy Editions, London 1994.

Hilary Cottam, *Radical Help: How We Can Remake the Relationships Between Us and Revolutionise the Welfare State*, Virago, London 2018.

Elizabeth Crawford, *Enterprising Women: The Garretts and their Circle*, Francis Boule Publishers, London 2002/2009.

Caroline Criado Perez, *Invisible Women: Exposing Data Bias in a World Designed for Men*, Chatto & Windus, London, 2019

David Crowley, Jane Pavitt (eds.), *Cold War Modern: Design 1945–1970*, exh. cat., V&A Publishing, London 2008.

Charles Darwin, *The Descent of Man: Selection in Relation to Sex* (1871), Penguin Classics, London 2004.

Charles Darwin, *The Origin of Species* (1859), Wordsworth Classics of World Literature, Ware 1998.

Chris Dercon, Wilfried Kuehn, Armin Linke (eds.), *Carlo Mollino: Maniera Moderna*, Verlag Walther König, Cologne 2011.

Chris Dercon, Helen Sainsbury, Wolfgang Tillmans (eds.), *Wolfgang Tillmans*, exh. cat., Tate Publishing, London 2017.

Alexander Dorner, *Catalogue for Herbert Bayer Exhibition at the London Gallery* (April 8–May 1,1937), London Gallery, London 1937.

Henry Dreyfuss, *Designing for People*, Simon & Schuster, New York 1955.

Magdalena Droste, Manfred Ludewig, Bauhaus-Archiv (eds.), *Marcel Breuer Design*, Taschen, Cologne 1992.

Anthony Dunne, *Hertzian Tales: Electronic Products, Aesthetic Experience and Critical Design*, Royal College of Art Computer Related Design Research Studio, London 1999.

Sam Durant (ed.), *Black Panther: The Revolutionary Art of Emory Douglas*, Rizzoli International Publications, New York 2007.

George Dyson, *Turing's Cathedral: The Origins of the Digital Universe*, Allen Lane, London 2012.

George Eliot, *Middlemarch* (1874), Penguin Classics, London 1985.

Ignazia Favata, *Joe Colombo and Italian Design of the Sixties*, Thames & Hudson, London 1988.

Fulvio Ferrari, Napoleone Ferrari, *The Furniture of Carlo Mollino*, Phaidon Press, London 2006.

Beppe Finessi, Cristina Miglio (eds.), *Mendini: A cura di*, Maurizio Corraini, Mantova 2009.

Alberto Fiz (ed.), *Mendini Alchimie: Dal Controdesign alle Nuove Utopie*, Mondadori Electa, Milan 2010.

Alan Fletcher, *Picturing and Poeting*, Phaidon Press, London 2006.

Henry Ford, Samuel Crowther, *My Life and Work—An Autobiography of Henry Ford*, Doubleday, Page and Company, New York 1922.

Kate Forde (ed.), *Dirt: The Filthy Reality of Everyday Life*, Profile Books in association with the Wellcome Collection, London 2009.

Norman Foster (ed.), *Dymaxion Car: Buckminster Fuller*, Ivorypress, Madrid and London 2010.

Celina Fox, *The Arts of Industry in the Age of Enlightenment*, Yale University Press, New Haven, Connecticut 2009.

Nicholas Fox Weber (ed.), *A Beautiful Confluence: Anni and Josef Albers and the Latin American World*, The Josef and Anni Albers Foundation, Bethany, Connecticut 2015.

Nicholas Fox Weber, Pandora Tabatabai Asbaghi, *Anni Albers*, Guggenheim Museum Publications, New York 1999.

Nicholas Fox Weber, *The Bauhaus Group: Six Masters of Modernism*, Alfred A. Knopf, New York 2009.

Nicholas Fox Weber, Martin Filler, *Josef + Anni Albers: Designs for Living*, Merrell Publishers, London 2004.

Mark Frauenfelder, *The Computer*, Carlton Books, London 2005.

Arnd Friedrichs, Kerstin Finger (eds.), *The Infamous Chair: 220C Virus Monobloc*, Die Gestalten Verlag, Berlin 2010.

Alastair Fuad-Luke, *Design Activism: Beautiful Strangeness for a Sustainable World*, Earthscan, London 2009.

Naoto Fukasawa, Jasper Morrison, *Super Normal: Sensations of the Ordinary*, Lars Müller Publishers, Baden 2007.

Martino Gamper, *100 Chairs in 100 Days and its 100 Ways*, Dent-De-Leone, London 2007.

Katya García-Antón, Emily King, Christian Brandle, *Wouldn't it Be Nice … Wishful Thinking in Art and Design*, exh. cat., Centre d'Art Contemporain de Genève, Geneva 2007.

Simon Garfield, *Just My Type: A book About Fonts*, Profile Books, London 2010.

Ken Garland, *Mr Beck's Underground Map*, Capital Transport Publishing, Harrow 2008.

Philippe Garner, *Eileen Gray: Designer and Architect*, Taschen, Cologne 1993.

Siegfried Giedion, *The Key to Reality: What Ails Our Time? Catalogue for Constructivist Art Exhibition at the London Gallery* (July 12 to 31, 1937), London Gallery, London 1937.

Siegfried Giedion, *Space, Time and Architecture: The Growth of a New Tradition*, Harvard University Press, Cambridge, Massachusetts 1941.

James Gleick, *The Information: A History, A Theory, A Flood*, Fourth Estate, London 2012.

Andrea Gleiniger *The Chair No. 14 by Michael Thonet*, Verlag form, Frankfurt 1998.

Mark Godfrey (ed.), *Richard Hamilton*, exh. cat., Tate Publishing, London 2014.

Mark Godfrey, Zoe Whitley (eds.) *Soul of a Nation: Art in the Age of Black Power*, exh. cat., Tate Publishing, London 2017.

Robert Graves, *Greek Myths* (1955), Cassell/QPD, London 1991.

Adam Greenfield, *Radical Technologies: The Design of Everyday Life*, Verso, London 2017.

Jean-Pierre Greff (ed.), *AC/DC Contemporary Art, Contemporary Design*, Geneva University of Art and Design, Geneva 2008.

Thierry Grillet, Marie-Laure Jousset (eds.), *Ettore Sottsass*, exh. cat., Éditions du Centre Pompidou, Paris 1994.

Joost Grootens, *I Swear I Use No Art at All: 10 Years, 100 Books, 18,788 Pages of Book Design*, 010 Publishers, Rotterdam 2010.

Robert Grudin, *Design and Truth*, Yale University Press, New Haven, Connecticut 2010.

Martí Guixé, *Food Designing*, Maurizio Corraini, Mantova 2010.

Fritz Haeg, *Edible Estates: Attack on the Front Lawn, A Project by Fritz Haeg*, Metropolis Books, New York 2008.

Tanya Harrod, *The Last Sane Man, Michael Cardew: Modern Pots, Colonialism, and the Counterculture*, Yale University Press, New Haven, Connecticut 2012.

Tanya Harrod, *The Real Thing: Essays on Making in the Modern World*, Hyphen Press, London 2015.

Carla Hartmann, Eames Demetrios (eds.), *100 Quotes by Charles Eames*, Eames Office, Santa Monica, California 2007.

W. F. Haug, *Critique of Commodity Aesthetics: Appearance, Sexuality and Advertising in Capitalist Society* (1971), Polity Press, Cambridge 1986.

K. Michael Hays, Dana Miller (eds.), *Buckminster Fuller: Starting with the Universe*, exh. cat., Whitney Museum of American Art, New York 2008.

Jing He, *Tulip Pyramid—Copy and Identity*, Design Academy Eindhoven, Eindhoven 2016.

Steven Heller, *Paul Rand*, Phaidon Press, London 1999.

John Heskett, *Industrial Design*, Thames & Hudson, London 1980.

John Heskett, *Toothpicks & Logos: Design in Everyday Life*, Oxford University Press, Oxford 2002.

E. J. Hobsbawm, *Industry and Empire* (1968), Penguin Books, Harmondsworth 1982.

E. J. Hobsbawm, *The Age of Capital: 1848–1875* (1975), Abacus, London 1985.

Eric Hobsbawm, *The Age of Extremes: The Short Twentieth Century 1914–1991* (1994), Abacus, London 2008.

E. J. Hobsbawm, *The Age of Revolution: Europe 1789–1848* (1962), Abacus, London 1987.

Elaine S. Hochman, *Bauhaus: Crucible of Modernism*, Fromm International, New York 1997.

Andrew Hodges, *Alan Turing: The Enigma* (1983), Vintage, London 2012.

Jens Hoffmann, Claudia J. Nahson (eds.), *Roberto Burle Marx: Brazilian Modernist*, Yale University Press, New Haven, Connecticut 2016.

Anne Hollander, *Sex and Suits: The Evolution of Modern Dress* (1994), Claridge Press, Brinkworth 1998.

Lilli Hollein, Tina Thiel, *Vienna Design Week, Stadtarbeit, Ten Years of Design Featuring the City*, Umstaetter, Vienna 2016.

Richard Holmes, *The Age of Wonder: How the Romantic Generation Discovered the Beauty and Terror of Science*, Harper Collins, London 2008.

Catherine Ince, Lotte Johnson, *The World of Charles and Ray Eames*, Thames & Hudson, London 2016.

Reginald Isaacs, *Gropius: An Illustrated Biography of the Creator of the Bauhaus* (1983), Bullfinch Press, Boston 1991.

Walter Isaacson, *Steve Jobs*, Little Brown, London 2011.

Frederic Jameson, *Postmodernism or, The Cultural Logic of Late Capitalism*, Verso, London 1991.

Iva Janáková (ed.), *Ladislav Sutnar—Prague—New York—Design in Action*, Argo, Prague 2003.

Charles Jencks, Nathan Silver, *Adhocism: The Case for Improvisation* (1972), Doubleday & Company, New York 2013.

Philip Johnson, *Machine Art*, exh. cat., The Museum of Modern Art, New York 1934.

Philip Johnson, *Objects: 1900 and Today*, exh. cat., The Museum of Modern Art, New York 1933.

Steve Jones, *Darwin's Island: The Galapagos in the Garden of England*, Little, Brown, London 2009.

Cees W. de Jong (ed.), *Jan Tschichold: Master Typographer, His Life, Work & Legacy*, Thames & Hudson, London 2008.

Lorraine Justice, *China's Design Revolution*, The MIT Press, Cambridge, Massachusetts 2012.

Masaki Kanai (ed.), *Muji*, Rizzoli International Publications, New York 2010.

Edgar Kaufmann Jr., *Good Design*, exh. cat., The Museum of Modern Art, New York 1950.

Edgar Kaufmann Jr., *Organic Design in Home Furnishings*, exh., cat., The Museum of Modern Art, New York 1941.

Edgar Kaufmann Jr., *Prize Designs for Modern Furniture*, exh. cat., The Museum of Modern Art, New York 1950.

Alison Kelly (ed.), *The Story of Wedgwood* (1962), Faber & Faber, London 1975.

Gyorgy Kepes, *Language of Vision* (1944), Dover Publications, New York 1995.

Gyorgy Kepes (ed.), *Gyorgy Kepes: The MIT Years 1945–1977*, The MIT Press, Cambridge, Massachusetts 1978.

Yuko Kikuchi, *Japanese Modernisation and Mingei Theory: Cultural nationalism and Oriental Orientalism*, RoutledgeCurzon, London 2004.

Emily King (ed.), *Designed by Peter Saville*, Frieze, London 2003.

Emily King, *Robert Brownjohn: Sex and Typography*, Princeton Architectural Press, New York 2005.

Pat Kirkham, *Charles and Ray Eames: Designers of the Twentieth Century*, The MIT Press, Cambridge, Massachusetts 1995.

Pat Kirkham, *The Gendered Object*, Manchester University Press, Manchester 1996.

Klaus Klemp, Hehn-Chu Ahn, Matthias Wagner K, *Korea Power—Design and Identity*, Gestalten, Berlin 2013.

Naomi Klein, *No Logo*, Flamingo, London 2000.

Anniina Koivu (ed.), *Ronan & Erwan Bouroullec: Works*, Phaidon Press, London 2012.

Rem Koolhaas, Bruce Mau with Jennifer Sigler (eds.). *Small, Medium, Large, Extra-Large: Office for Metropolitan Architecture*, 010 Publishers, Rotterdam 1995.

Rem Koolhaas, Hans Ulrich Obrist, *Project Japan: Metabolism Talks …* , Taschen, Cologne 2011.

Joachim Krausse, Claude Lichtenstein (eds.), *Your Private Sky: R. Buckminster Fuller*, Lars Müller Publishers, Baden 2000.

Mateo Kries, Jochen Eisenbrand, (eds.), *Alexander Girard: A Designer's Universe*, exh. cat., Vitra Design Museum, Weil-am-Rhein 2016.

Mateo Kries, Christoph Thun-Hohenstein, Amelie Klein, *Hello Robot: Design between Human and Machine*, exh. cat., Vitra Design Museum, Weil-am-Rhein 2017.

Mateo Kries, Alexander von Vegesack (eds.), *Joe Colombo: Inventing the Future*, exh. cat., Vitra Design Museum, Weil-am-Rhein 2005.

Max Lamb, *My Grandfather's Tree*, Dent-de-Leon, London 2015.

Yvon Lambert (ed.) *Cy Twombly. Catalogue raisonné des oeuvres sur papier. Vol. VI 1973–1966*, Multhipla Edizioni, Milan 1976.

Peter Lang, William Menking (eds.), *Superstudio: Life Without Objects*, Skira Editore, Milan 2003.

Andres Lepik, Ayça Beygo (eds.), *Francis Kéré: Radically Simple*, Hatje Cantz Verlag, Berlin 2016.

Jeremy Lewis, *Penguin Special: The Life and Times of Allen Lane* (2005), Penguin Books, London 2006.

William Little, H. W. Fowler, Jessie Coulson with C. T. Onions (ed.), *The Shorter Oxford English Dictionary On Historical Principles: Volume 1*, Clarendon Press, Oxford 1987.

Loretta Lorance, *Becoming Bucky Fuller*, The MIT Press, Cambridge, Massachusetts 2009.

Sophie Lovell, *Dieter Rams: As Little Design as Possible*, Phaidon Press, London 2011.

Jacques Lucan (ed.), *OMA—Rem Koolhaas: Architecture 1970–1990* (1990), Princeton Architectural Press, New York 1991.

Fiona MacCarthy, *The Last Pre-Raphaelite: Edward Burne-Jones and the Victorian Imagination*, Faber & Faber, London 2011.

Fiona MacCarthy, *William Morris: A Life for Our Time*, Faber & Faber, London 1994.

Christine Macel, *Viva Arte Viva: 57th International Art Exhibition La Biennale Di Venezia*, exh. cat., Rizzoli International Publications, New York 2017.

John Maeda with Becky Bermont *Redesigning Leadership: Design, Technology, Business, Life*, The MIT Press, Cambridge, Massachusetts 2011.

Karl Mang, *History of Modern Furniture*, Verlag Gerd Hatje, Stuttgart 1978.

Beate Manske (ed.), *Wilhelm Wagenfeld (1900–1990)*, Hatje Cantz Verlag, Ostfildern-Ruit 2000.

Ank Leeuw Marcar (ed.), *Willem Sandberg—Portrait of an Artist*, Valiz, Amsterdam 2014.

Bruce Mau, *Life Style*, Phaidon Press, London 2000.

Bruce Mau and the Institute without Boundaries, *Massive Change*, Phaidon Press, London 2004.

Cara McCarty, *Designs for Independent Living*, exh. cat., The Museum of Modern Art, New York 1988.

Mary McLeod (ed.), *Charlotte Perriand: An Art of Living*, Harry N. Abrams, New York 2003.

Christien Meindertsma, *Pig 05049*, Flocks, Rotterdam 2007.

Metahaven, Marina Vishmidt (eds.), *Uncorporate Identity*, Lars Müller Publishers/Jan van Eyck Academie, Baden/Maastricht 2010.

Bill Moggridge, *Designing Interactions*, The MIT Press, Cambridge, Massachusetts 2007.

Bill Moggridge, *Designing Media*, The MIT Press, Cambridge, Massachusetts 2010.

László Moholy-Nagy, *Vision in Motion*, Paul Theobald & Co., Chicago 1947.

Sibyl Moholy-Nagy, *Moholy-Nagy: Experiment in Totality*, Harper & Brothers, New York 1950.

Anne Montfort (ed.), *Sonia Delaunay*, exh. cat., Tate Enterprises, London 2014.

Richard Morphet (ed.), *Richard Hamilton*, exh. cat., Tate Gallery Publications, London 1992.

Jasper Morrison, *A Book of Spoons*, Imschoot Uitgevers, Ghent 1997.

Jasper Morrison, *A Book of Things*, Lars Müller Publishers, Zurich 2015.

Jasper Morrison, *Everything but the Walls*, Lars Müller Publishers, Baden 2002.

Jasper Morrison, *The Good Life: Perceptions of the Ordinary*, Lars Müller Publishers, Zurich 2014.

Jasper Morrison, *The Hard Life*, Lars Müller Publishers, Zurich 2017.

Farshid Moussavi, *The Function of Form*, Actar/Harvard University Graduate School of Design, Barcelona/Cambridge, Massachusetts 2009.

Farshid Moussavi, Michael Kubo (eds.), *The Function of Ornament*, Actar, Barcelona 2006.

Farshid Moussavi, *The Function of Style*, Actar, Barcelona 2015.

Bruno Munari, *Design as Art* (1966), Penguin Books, London 2008.

Bruno Munari, *Supplemento al dizionario italiano/Supplement to the Italian dictionary* (1963), Maurizio Corraini, Mantova 2004.

Heike Munder (ed.), *Peter Saville Estate 1–127*, migros museum für gegenwartskunst Zürich/JRP|Ringier, Zurich 2007.

John Neuhart, Marilyn Neuhart, Ray Eames, *Eames Design: The Work of the Office of Charles and Ray Eames*, Thames and Hudson, London 1989.

Marilyn Neuhart with John Neuhart, *The Story of Eames Furniture*, Gestalten, Berlin 2010.

Marie Neurath, Robert S. Cohen (eds.), *Otto Neurath: Empiricism and Sociology*, D. Reidel Publishing Company, Dordecht 1973.

Otto Neurath, *From Hieroglyphics to Isotype: A Visual Autobiography*, Hyphen Press, London 2010.

Jocelyn de Noblet (ed.), *Design, miroir du siècle*, Flammarion/APCI, Paris 1993.

Hans Ulrich Obrist (ed.), *A Brief History of Curating*, JRP|Ringier, Zurich 2008.

Hans Ulrich Obrist, Asad Raza, *Ways of Curating*, Allen Lane, London 2015.

Jonathan Olivares, *A Taxonomy of the Office Chair*, Phaidon, London 2011.

Victor Papanek, *Design for the Real World: Human Ecology and Social Change* (1971), Academy Chicago Publishers, Chicago 1985.

Rozsika Parker, *The Subversive Stitch: Embroidery and the Making of the Feminine*, The Women's Press, London 1984.

Martin Pawley, *Buckminster Fuller: How Much Does the Building Weigh?* (1990), Trefoil Publications, London 1995.

Alejandra de la Paz, Virginia Ruano (eds.), *Clara Porset's Design: Creating a Modern Mexico*, Museo Franz Mayer, Mexico City 2006.

Charlotte Perriand, *Charlotte Perriand: A Life of Creation*, The Monacelli Press, New York 2003.

Ingrid Pfeiffer, Max Hollein (eds.), *László Moholy-Nagy Retrospective*, Prestel, Munich and Berlin 2009.

Emily Pilloton, *Design Revolution: 100 Products That Empower People*, Metropolis Books, New York 2009.

Plato, *The Republic*, trans. Desmond Lee 1995, Penguin Books, London 2007.

Paul Polak, *Out of Poverty: What Works When Traditional Approaches Fail*, Berrett-Koehler Publishers, San Francisco 2008.

Sergio Polano, *Achille Castiglioni: Tutte le opere 1938–2000*, Electa, Milan 2001.

Lisa Licitra Ponti, *Gio Ponti: The Complete Work 1923–1978*, Thames & Hudson, London 1990.

Jane Portal (ed.), *The First Emperor: China's Terracotta Army*, exh. cat., The British Museum Press, London 2007.

Rick Poynor (ed.), *Communicate: Independent British Graphic Design since the Sixties*, exh. cat., Barbican Art Gallery/Laurence King Publishing, London 2004.

Rick Poynor, *No More Rules: Graphic Design and Postmodernism*, Laurence King Publishing, London 2003.

Graham Pullin, *Design Meets Disability*, The MIT Press, Cambridge, Massachusetts 2009.

Barbara Radice, *Ettore Sottsass: A Critical Biography*, Rizzoli International Publications, New York 1993.

Dieter Rams, *Less but Better*, Jo Klatt Design+Design Verlag, Hamburg 1995.

Herbert Read, *Art and Industry*, Faber & Faber, London 1934.

Casey Reas, Ben Fry, *Processing: A Programming Handbook for Visual Designers and Artists*, The MIT Press, Cambridge, Massachusetts 2007.

Casey Reas, Chandler McWilliams, LUST, *Form + Code: In Design, Art and Architecture*, Princeton Architectural Press, New York 2010.

Peter Reed (ed.), *Alvar Aalto: Between Humanism and Materialism*, exh.cat., The Museum of Modern Art, New York 1998.

David Reinfurt, Robert Wiesenberger, *Muriel Cooper*, The MIT Press, Cambridge, Massachusetts 2017.

Timo de Rijk, *Norm = Form on standardisation and design*, Foundation Design den Haag/Gemeentemuseum Den Haag/Uitgeverij Thieme Art b.v., Deventer, The Hague 2010.

Terence Riley, Barry Bergdoll (eds.), *Mies in Berlin*, exh. cat., The Museum of Modern Art, New York 2001.

Jose Roca, Alejandro Martin, *Waterweavers: A Chronicle of Rivers*, Bard Graduate Center, New York 2014.

Marco Romanelli, *Gio Ponti: A World*, Editrice Abitare Segesta, Milan 2002

Catharine Rossi, Alex Coles (eds.), *EP/Volume. 1: The Italian Avant-Garde, 1968–1976*, Sternberg Press, Berlin 2013.

David Rothenberg, *Survival of the Beautiful: Art, Science, and Evolution*, Bloomsbury Press, New York 2011.

Bernard Rudofsky, *Architecture Without Architects: A Short Introduction to Non-Pedigreed Architecture* (1964), University of New Mexico Press, Albuquerque, New Mexico 1987.

Zoë Ryan (ed.), *As Seen: Exhibitions that Made Architececture and Design History*, The Art Institute of Chicago, Chicago 2017.

ZoUe Ryan, Joseph Rosa, *Hyperlinks: Architecture and Design*, The Art Institute of Chicago, Chicago 2010.

Louise Schouwenberg, *Hella Jongerius*, Phaidon Press, London 2003.

Louise Schouwenberg (ed.), *Hella Jongerius: Misfit*, Phaidon Press, London 2010.

Sarah Schrauwen, Lucienne Roberts, Rebecca Wright (eds.), *Can Graphic Design Save Your Life?* GraphicDesign&, London 2017.

Franz Schulze, *Philip Johnson: Life and Work*, Alfred A. Knopf, New York 1994.

Sabine Schulze, Ina Grätz (eds.), *Apple Design*, Hatje Cantz Verlag, Ostfildern-Ruit 2011.

Lella Secor Florence, *Our Private Lives: America and Britain*, George G. Harrap, London 1944.

Meryle Secrest, *Frank Lloyd Wright: A Biography*, Alfred A. Knopf, New York 1992.

Richard Sennett, *The Conscience of the Eye: The Design and Social Life of Cities*, Alfred A. Knopf, New York 1990.

Richard Sennett, *The Craftsman*, Allen Lane, London 2008.

Paul Shaw, *Helvetica and the New York City Subway System: The True (Maybe) Story*, The MIT Press, Cambridge, Massachusetts 2010.

Malkit Shoshan, *Atlas of the Conflict: Israel—Palestine*, 010 Publishers, Amsterdam 2013.

Samuel Smiles, *Josiah Wedgwood, FRS: His Personal* (1895), Leopold Classic Library, South Yarra 2016.

Patti Smith, *Just Kids* Bloomsbury Publishing, London 2010.

Félix Solaguren-Beascoa de Corral, *Arne Jacobsen*, Editorial Gustavo Gili, Barcelona 1991.

Leendert Sonnevelt, Job Melhuizen, *Dutch Design Today: Be the Future/Back to the Future*, Lecturis, Eindhoven 2017.

Susan Sontag (ed.), *Barthes: Selected Writings*, Fontana Paperbacks, London 1983.

Penny Sparke (ed.), Reyner Banham, *Design by Choice*, Academy Editions, London 1981.

Penny Sparke, *Italian Design: 1870 to the Present*, Thames and Hudson, London 1988.

Nancy Spector (ed.), *Matthew Barney: The Cremaster Cycle*, Harry N. Abrams, New York 2002.

Alex Steffen (ed.), *Worldchanging: A User's Guide for the 21st Century*, Harry N. Abrams Inc., New York 2006.

Kate Stohr, Cameron Sinclair (eds.), *Design Like You Give A Damn: Architectural Responses to Humanitarian Crises*, Metropolis Books, New York 2006.

Nina Stritzler-Levine (ed.), *Sheila Hicks: Weaving as Metaphor*, Yale University Press, New Haven, Connecticut 2006.

Swapnaa Tamhane, Rashmi Varma, *Sār: The Essence of Indian Design*, Phaidon Press, London 2016.

Bobbye Tigerman (ed.), *A Handbook of California Design, 1930–1965: Craftspeople, Designers, Manufacturers*, Los Angeles County Museum of Art/The MIT Press, Los Angeles/Cambridge, Massachusetts 2013.

Van Dale Groot woordenboek van de Nederlandse taal, Van Dale, Utrecht 2015.

Arjen Van Susteren, *Metropolitan World Atlas*, 010 Publishers, Amsterdam 2004.

Frederick Winslow Taylor, *The Principles of Scientific Management* (1911), Dover Publications, Mineola, New York 2003.

Henk Tennekes, *The Simple Science of Flight: From Insects to Jumbo Jets*, The MIT Press, Cambridge, Massachusetts 2009.

John Thackara (ed.), *Design After Modernism: Beyond the Object*, Thames & Hudson, London 1988.

John Thackara, *In the Bubble: Designing in a Complex World*, The MIT Press, Cambridge, Massachusetts 2006.

Wolfgang Tillmans, *If One Thing Matters, Everything Matters*, Tate Publishing, London 2003.

Frank Trentmann, *Empire of Things*, Allen Lane, London 2016.

Edward Tufte, *Beautiful Evidence*, Graphics Press, Cheshire, Connecticut 2006.

Edward R. Tufte, *Envisioning Information*, Graphics Press, Cheshire, Connecticut 1990.

Edward R. Tufte, *The Visual Display of Quantitative Information* (1983), Graphics Press, Cheshire, Connecticut 2001.

Margarita Tupitsyn (ed.), *Rodchenko and Popova: Defining Constructivism*, exh. cat., Tate Publishing, London 2009.

Keiko Ueki-Polet, Klaus Kemp (eds.), *Less and More: The Design Ethos of Dieter Rams*, Die Gestalten Verlag, Berlin 2009.

Jenny Uglow, *The Lunar Men: The Friends who Made the Future 1730–1810*, Faber and Faber, London 2002.

Jenny Uglow, *The Pinecone: The Story of Sarah Losh, Forgotten Romantic Heroine – Antiquarian, Architect and Visionary*, Faber and Faber, London 2012.

Giorgio Vasari, *Lives of the Artists: Volume I* (1550), Penguin Books, London 1987.

Alexander von Vegesack, *Thonet: Classic Furniture in Bent Wood and Tubular Steel*, Hazar Publishing, London 1996.

Robert Venturi, Denise Scott Brown, Steven Izenour, *Learning from Las Vegas: The Forgotten Symbolism of Architectural Form* (1972), The MIT Press, Cambridge, Massachusetts 1977.

Lukas Verweij (ed.), *Hella Jongerius: I Don't Have a Favorite Colour, Creating the Vitra Colour & Material Library*, Gestalten, Berlin 2016.

Peter Weiss (ed.), *Alessandro Mendini: Design and Architecture*, Electa, Milan 2001.

Eyal Weizman, *Forensic Architecture: Violence at the Threshold of Detectability*, The MIT Press, Cambridge, Massachusetts 2017.

Nigel Whiteley, *Reyner Banham: Historian of the Immediate Future*, The MIT Press, Cambridge, Massachusetts 2002.

Raymond Williams, *Keywords: A Vocabulary of Culture and Society* (1976), Fontana, London 1983.

Elizabeth Wilson, *Adorned in Dreams: Fashion and Modernity*, Virago Press, London 1985.

Elizabeth Wilson, *Hallucinations: Life in the Post-Modern City* (1988), Hutchinson Radius, London 1989.

Hans M. Wingler, *Bauhaus: Weimar, Dessau, Berlin, Chicago*, The MIT Press, Cambridge, Massachusetts 1976.

Sōetsu Yanagi, *The Unknown Craftsman: A Japanese Insight into Beauty*, Kodansha International, Tokyo 1972.

Theodore Zeldin, *An Intimate History of Humanity* (1994), Vintage, London 1998.

Ida van Zijl, *Droog Design 199–1996*, Centraal Museum, Utrecht 1997.

Index of Names

About the Author

Alice Rawsthorn is an award-winning design critic and author, whose weekly design column for *The New York Times* was syndicated worldwide for over a decade. From 2014 to 2017 she wrote the *By Design* column for *frieze* magazine. Her previous books include the critically acclaimed *Hello World: Where Design Meets Life.* Born in Manchester and based in London, Rawsthorn speaks on design at global events including TED and the World Economic Forum's annual meeting in Davos. She is chair of the boards of trustees of Chisenhale Gallery in London and The Hepworth Wakefield gallery in Yorkshire. A founding member of the Writers for Liberty campaign to champion human rights, Rawsthorn was awarded an Order of the British Empire (OBE) for services to design and the arts.

Acknowledgments

The first person I must thank for their help with this book is Jennifer Higgie, editorial director of *frieze*. When we discussed my writing a design column for *frieze* five years ago, Jennifer suggested that I should plan it with the objective of publishing all of the columns together as a book. I have since written new texts for *Design as an Attitude*, and the original columns have been expanded and updated, but the book would not have existed without Jennifer. I am deeply grateful to her for the idea and for her support as an exceptionally generous and inspiring editor. Thank you too to everyone else at *frieze*.

I must also thank another generous and inspiring friend, Hans Ulrich Obrist, for introducing me to Clément Dirié, who has published *Design as an Attitude* as part of JRP|Editions' *Documents* series. It has been a pleasure to work with Clément and his team at JRP|Editions and their international distributors. I am immensely grateful to all of them, as well as to my literary agent Toby Mundy and his colleagues at TMA, and to Caitlin Allen, Katy MacMillan-Scott, and Preena Gadher of Riot Communications.

My thanks are due to the staff of the institutions where I conducted research for the book: the National Art Library at the Victoria & Albert Museum in London and the Museum Library of The Museum of Modern Art in New York.

I am also thankful to all of the individuals and organizations that have so kindly allowed us to use their images in *Design as an Attitude*: Gianni Antoniali; Joan Bardeletti; Blackhorse Workshop; Marco Beck Peccoz; Peter Biľak; Irma Boom; Chisenhale Gallery, London; Danish Crafts; Fairphone; Fuseproject; Marcus Gaab; Martino Gamper; Jeppe Gudmundsen; Jing He; Camille Henrot; Andy Keate; Chris Liljenberg Halstrøm; Hella Jongerius and JongeriusLab; Alan Karchmer; KLM Royal Dutch Airlines; Marc Latzel; Michael Leckie; Gabriel A. Maher; Matteo de Mayda; Memphis srl; National Museum of African American History and Culture, Washington DC; Maureen Paley; Laura Pana

and Migrationlab; Peek; Jan Willem Petersen and Specialist
Operations; Travis Rathbone; Femke Reijerman; Rolex
Awards; Sehat Kahani; Studio Azzuro; Studio Formafantasma;
Talking Hands; The Ocean Cleanup; Wolfgang Tillmans;
Toca Boca; Faye Toogood; Arthur Zang; and Erwin Zwart.

Design as an Attitude is the product of many years of research
into design. I have been incredibly lucky to have been helped
in that process by colleagues at *The New York Time*s, and
by all of the other friends and collaborators who share my
passion for design, or have contributed in other ways. I owe
them all a huge debt, personally and professionally, as I do
to the wonderful designers, makers, fixers, engineers, coders,
artists, architects, writers, curators, historians, and people
from other fields, who have been so generous in sharing
their knowledge and experiences of design with me. Some
of them appear in *Design as an Attitude*, and others have
influenced the book by informing my thinking on design.
With love and thanks to you all.

Imprint

EDITOR
Clément Dirié

EDITORIAL ASSISTANCE
Jessica Bourgoz

COPY EDITING AND PROOFREADING
Clare Manchester

DESIGN CONCEPT
Gavillet & Cie, Geneva

DESIGN
Nicolas Leuba, Nicolas Eigenheer

PRINT AND BINDING
Musumeci S.p.A., Quart (Aosta)

TYPEFACE
Genath (www.optimo.ch)

PUBLISHED BY
JRP | Editions
Rue des Bains 39
CH–1205 Geneva
info@jrp-editions.com
www.jrp-editions.com

IN CO-EDITION WITH
Les presses du réel
35, rue Colson
F–21000 Dijon
info@lespressesdureel.com
www.lespressesdureel.com

ISBN 978-3-03764-521-5 (JRP | Editions)
ISBN 978-2-84066-984-5 (Les presses du réel)

Distribution

JRP | Editions publications are available internationally
at selected bookstores and from the following distribution
partners:

GERMANY AND AUSTRIA
Vice Versa Distribution GmbH
www.viceversaartbooks.com

FRANCE
Les presses du réel
www.lespressesdureel.com

SWITZERLAND
AVA Verlagsauslieferung AG
www.ava.ch

UK AND OTHER EUROPEAN COUNTRIES
Cornerhouse Publications, HOME
www.cornerhousepublications.org

USA, CANADA, ASIA, AND AUSTRALIA
ARTBOOK | D. A. P.
www.artbook.com

For a list of our partner bookshops or for any general
questions, please contact JRP | Editions directly at
info@jrp-editions.com, or visit our homepage
www.jrp-editions.com for further information.

Documents Series 28:
Alice Rawsthorn
Design as an Attitude

This book is the twenty-eighth
volume in the "Documents" series,
dedicated to critics' writings.

The series was founded by
Lionel Bovier and Xavier Douroux.

Also available

DOCUMENTS SERIES (IN ENGLISH)

John Baldessari, *More Than You Wanted to Know About John Baldessari*
ISBN 978-3-03764-192-7 (JRP | Ringier) [*Vol. 1*]
ISBN 978-3-03764-256-6 (JRP | Ringier) [*Vol. 2*]

Cristina Bechtler & Dora Imhof,
The Private Museum of the Future
ISBN 978-3-03764-520-8 (JRP | Ringier)
ISBN 978-2-84066-983-8 (Les presses du réel)

Sarah Burkhalter & Laurence Schmidlin,
Spacescapes. Dance & Drawing since 1962
ISBN 978-3-03764-469-0 (JRP | Ringier)
ISBN 978-2-84066-917-3 (Les presses du réel)

Gabriele Detterer & Maurizio Nannucci, *Artist-Run Spaces*
ISBN 978-3-03764-191-0 (JRP | Ringier)
ISBN 978-2-84066-512-0 (Les presses du réel)

Tim Griffin, *Writings on Wade Guyton*
ISBN 978-3-03764-473-7 (JRP | Ringier)
ISBN 978-2-84066-945-6 (Les presses du réel)

Hans Ulrich Obrist, *A Brief History of Curating*
ISBN 978-3-905829-55-6 (JRP | Ringier)
ISBN 978-2-84066-287-7 (Les presses du réel)

Hans Ulrich Obrist, *A Brief History of New Music*
ISBN 978-3-03764-190-3 (JRP | Ringier)
ISBN 978-2-84066-619-6 (Les presses du réel)

Tomás Pospiszyl, *An Associative Art History*
ISBN 978-3-03764-517-8 (JRP | Ringier)
ISBN 978-2-84066-982-1 (Les presses du réel)